Penguin Books
Apartheid and Internationa

Keith Ovenden is a freelance writer and political analyst, well known both in Australia and the northern hemisphere for his commentaries on contemporary affairs. He was educated at the Universities of Keele, Michigan, and Oxford, where he was awarded his doctorate. In addition to his widely praised policy study of the British steel industry (The Politics of Steel), he has also published two novels, *Ratatui* and *O.E.*, and contributed to many leading publications, including the London *Financial Times*.

He is married to the economist Helen Sutch, and, with their two children, manages to live some of the time at their home in Wellington, New Zealand.

Tony Cole studied economics at the University of Sydney, and joined the Treasury in 1968. From 1980 to 1983 he was Alternate Executive Director of the World Bank in Washington, DC, representing Australia, South Korea, New Zealand, Papua New Guinea and several smaller Pacific Island countries. In 1983 he became Senior Private Secretary to Treasurer Paul Keating, and in 1985 the Minister (Economic) at the Australian High Commission in London. In 1987 he returned to Australia to work in the Prime Minister's Department, where he is currently Deputy Secretary.

He is married, and enjoys surfing, tennis, reading and cooking.

Apartheid and International Finance

A Program for Change

**Keith Ovenden
and
Tony Cole**

Penguin Books

Penguin Books Australia Ltd
487 Maroondah Highway, PO Box 257
Ringwood, Victoria, 3134, Australia
Penguin Books Ltd
Harmondsworth, Middlesex, England
Viking Penguin Inc.
40 West 23rd Street, New York, NY 10010, USA
Penguin Books Canada Limited
2801 John Street, Markham, Ontario, Canada, L3R 1B4
Penguin Books (N.Z.) Ltd
182-190 Wairau Road, Auckland 10, New Zealand

First published by Penguin Books Australia, 1989

Typeset in 10/12pt Andover by Midland Typesetters, Maryborough, Vic.
Made and printed in Australia by The Book Printer, Maryborough, Vic.

CIP

Ovenden, Keith
Apartheid and international finance – a program for change.
Bibliography.
Includes index.
ISBN 0 14 012835 2.
1. Apartheid. 2. International economic relations. 3. International finance.
I. Cole, Tony (Tony S.). II. Title.
320.5'6

Umntu ungumntu ngabanye abantu
A person is a person by means of other people
(African proverb)

Contents

Contents

List of Figures and Tables

Authors' Note

Quite a lot of this book is about money and the uses to which it can be put. South African money, the Rand, has changed in value so much over the past ten years that its value may be difficult for outsiders to grasp. Measured against a basket of currencies of South Africa's principal trading partners, the Rand depreciated from an index of 100 on 24 January 1979 to 45.8 at the same time in 1989. Since then it has sunk some more. In 1981 US$1 would purchase 87.75 South African cents. In January 1989 it would purchase R2.38 – almost a threefold increase. This, however, is only the Commercial Rand. There is also the Financial Rand, which traded (in January 1989) at a discount of 38.9% to the Commercial Rand.

One of our intentions is to try to make the obscurities of South Africa's two-tier exchange rate more clear. As a rule of thumb, and if you need to make comparisons, the Rand was worth approximately US$1 in 1982 and US$0.50 throughout 1987 and the first two months of 1988.

Much of the material in this book was supplied to us by members of the international financial community. In the nature of things, their co-operation with us was in confidence, but we would like to take this opportunity to express publicly our gratitude to them for their generous assistance. In banking, time really is money.

Keith Ovenden and Tony Cole
Canberra, 13 June 1989

Foreword

Between 1984 and 1986, as the whole world knows, South Africa went through another terrible period of violence, repression and bloodshed. Campaigning for their rights, and for recognition of their legitimate political aspirations, the ordinary black people of South Africa once again found themselves confronted with the brutality of the organised racism of apartheid. The crisis of political legitimacy of which these events were an expression continues to this day.

What is possibly less well known is that ever since 1985, but as a direct result of the events of that year, South Africa has been experiencing another crisis, one that also shows no sign of abating. This is the crisis of the regime's links to international finance, and their relationship in turn to the underlying economic weaknesses of South African society. What happened was that in July and August of 1985 international financial institutions, beginning in New York, declined to roll over the loans that they had made available to their various South African clients, and which were due for repayment. South Africa had become an unacceptable risk, both because of its own domestic turbulence, and because of the increasing pressure that finance houses were experiencing from clients, shareholders and the general public in their own countries.

The quantity of loans requiring repayment was in excess of the ability of the South African economy, increasingly weakened by apartheid policies, to pay. The result was a foreign exchange crisis. South Africa was forced to close its exchanges for four days at the end of August 1985, to reintroduce exchange controls of various kinds, and to declare a moratorium on a proportion of its international debt. Since then, and as a direct result of these actions, South Africa has been excluded from international capital markets for anything other than short-term loans. It cannot raise capital to cover a balance of payments deficit should it run one. Its companies and corporations cannot borrow internationally to finance development. Four years on, though it has had two interim agreements on short-term rescheduling of its debt obligations, the regime still has no solution to its financial problem, and is faced with the need either to renegotiate the debt repayments that fall due in June 1990 (approximately US$14 billion in loans and bonds) or to be in default.

In this book Keith Ovenden and Tony Cole build on work that was originally commissioned through the Commonwealth Foreign Ministers' Committee on Southern Africa. The committee was set up by the Commonwealth Heads of Government when they gathered in Vancouver in October 1987. At its meetings, held every six months over the past two years, the committee has maintained a watching brief on developments in the southern African region, and commissioned research and analysis of developments. The committee will report on its work to the Commonwealth governments in Kuala Lumpur in October. It was at the request of the Vancouver meeting of Commonwealth Heads of Government that the committee asked for an officials' report on South Africa's links with international finance, and which then decided, in the wake of that report, to accept an Australian initiative to bring the work to the attention of international opinion by having it updated and recast.

The fruits of that labour are in this book. Keith Ovenden and Tony Cole explain what the international financial 'sanction' that has been in place since 1985 means. They illustrate its effects and explain its consequences. They show why it must be retained and, in places, tightened. They confirm that the pressures exerted by churches, anti-apartheid groups and other decent opinion throughout the Western world have played an indispensable part in ensuring that apartheid cannot now appeal to international finance to save it.

All the peoples of the Commonwealth, united in their condemnation of apartheid and in their desire to see it replaced with self-determination for all the citizens of South Africa, will want to try to ensure that a development as important as this will be sustained.

We also have a common interest in trying to ensure that the message contained in this book gains the attention of as wide an international public as possible.

I fear that it is perhaps common for us, in the context of the appalling character of apartheid, to be preoccupied with moral and humanitarian matters to the exclusion of the somewhat drier material from 'the dismal science' of economics. The tendency is understandable. Apartheid, for the ordinary black people of South Africa, means a daily struggle with racism, poverty and repression, injustice and deprivation. Perhaps economists have not done enough to bring these issues alive for us through the conceptual apparatus of their own discipline.

This book is therefore doubly welcome. It reminds us, with rigorous analysis written in accessible prose, that the daily experiences of the black majority have some of their origins in the economic structures of apartheid, but that they also have consequences for the functioning of the economy of apartheid as a whole. It is a timely reminder, not least because it can help us to take heart and to keep hope. Apartheid is not only the enemy of humanity: it is its own enemy as well, containing the seeds of its own economic destruction. The nurturing of those seeds is another of the tasks to which the Commonwealth must devote its energies, in tandem, to be sure, with the continuing efforts and struggles of all the courageous peoples of South Africa.

Shridath Ramphal
Commonwealth Secretary-General

Abbreviations

ANC	African National Congress
BIS	Bank for International Settlements
CAAA	Comprehensive Anti-Apartheid Act (USA)
CFMSA	Commonwealth Foreign Ministers' Committee on Southern Africa
EEC	European Economic Community
EPG	Eminent Persons Group
FRG	Federal Republic of Germany
GDP	Gross Domestic Product
GNP	Gross National Product
GST	General Sales Tax
IBRD	International Bank for Reconstruction and Development
IDA	International Development Association
IDASA	Institute for a Democratic Alternative in South Africa
IFC	International Finance Corporation
IMF	International Monetary Fund
IRRC	Investor Responsibility Research Centre
LDCs	Less Developed Countries
LIBOR	London Inter-bank Offer Rates: prevailing rates of interest for loans between major banks in London
MBOs	Management Buy-Outs

MNR	Renamo, the Mozambique National Resistance
Numsa	National Union of Metalworkers of South Africa
OECD	Organisation for Economic Co-operation and Development
PIC	Public Investment Commission (South Africa)
SADCC	Southern African Development Co-ordination Conference
SADF	South African Defence Force
SARB	South African Reserve Bank
SDR	Special Drawing Rights: a unit of value employed by the IMF based on a basket of major currencies
TBVC	Transkei, Bophuthatswana, Venda and Ciskei: the four independent homelands
UDF	United Democratic Front
UN	United Nations
VAT	Value Added Tax

CHAPTER ONE

Introduction

Apartheid is synonymous with waste: the waste of human potential and human resources.

Economics is the discipline of production, savings and growth: the employment of resources and of talent for the creation of wealth.

The two are poles apart. But whereas apartheid can make no contribution to any of the human sciences, the human sciences can help us not only to understand apartheid, but to defeat it.

There have been many political, sociological and historical accounts of apartheid, and what has been done to the peoples of southern Africa in its name. There have been great novels that have expressed the triumph of the human will, and its capacity to survive the violence and destruction that apartheid has wrought on all its peoples: tormented and tormentors alike.

Yet the characteristic fields of economics: labour, the allocation of resources, trade, investment, productivity, consumption, supply and demand: these have all too rarely been mobilised for the analysis and discussion of one of the great and tragic problems of our age.

This is a book about some aspects of just one relationship between apartheid and a field in which the discipline of economics can provide illumination: international finance capital. Its focus is an unconventional and at first glance, perhaps, surprising one – the international links that exist between South Africa and the great financial institutions of the Western world: banks, international agencies, individual governments, and government bodies of various kinds. The topic may be surprising because, with the exception of some few international economists, public interest in international finance capital and its relations with South Africa has generally been the preserve of a rather unrewarding kind of blunt Marxism: one in which the equation of racial segregation and repression, and the political hegemony of white South Africa, has been drawn as a twisted response to the pursuit of class interests. In this formulation, international finance capital – a disembodied abstract term that seems unconnected with any particular institutions or people – is simply banker to and for the class interests of the bourgeoisie.

We should begin by saying that we do not believe that this approach can contribute much to an understanding of the current critical state of the political economy of South Africa. Nor do we believe that it will be helpful in analysing the relations – both those that do and those that do not exist – between South Africans and the institutions of international finance.

The South African economy is complex, with a number of notable features that make it so unlike anywhere else in the world that studying it seems sometimes more akin to astronomy than to the human sciences. For a supposedly developing country on the capitalist model it has a substantial public sector accounting for approximately 28% of GDP. For a country with no obvious competing power anywhere in its geographical sphere of influence, it supports armed services that account for 20% of its anuual budget, and 5% of GNP, and that could, in extremis, call on the trained services of 425,000 men. (The figures are for 1986. Baynham, in Blumenfeld 1987b, 117.) And in addition to the size and 'firepower' of its public sector, the South African state has added a range and degree of regulatory interventionism, particularly in its labour and capital markets, its foreign exchange regime, and its systems of justice and social control, that are in excess of anything imposed in any other Western society.

In a country whose political leaders have made it an axiomatic article of faith over many years that the 'outside' world should not interfere in its affairs, there has grown up the largest international commercial cartel since Spain tried to corner the market in Mexican gold. The Central Selling Organisation of de Beers, part of the complex web of companies that embraces E. Oppenheimer and Son, the Anglo-American Corporation, de Beers Consolidated Mines, and all their many subsidiaries and agencies both in southern Africa and around the world, has by a combination of manipulation, financial and political pressure, and the control of resources, fixed the world price of diamonds for decades.

In a country rich in mineral wealth beyond the dreams of Croesus, where a tenth of the population leads a way of life equal in its wealth and opportunity to the conditions prevailing anywhere in the developed world, there exists a degree of poverty and human deprivation that many of us in the West would probably find hard to believe unless we saw it with our own eyes. And more. Much of this poverty and deprivation is a direct consequence of the policy of apartheid.

In a country which for the great bulk of this century has been regarded in official circles in the West as a part of the capitalist world economy, the politics of race have introduced distortions and the misallocation of resources on a scale that is now making for most interesting developments.

There is much that is unusual and striking about the political economy of South Africa. So too is there much that is interesting in the complex character of international financial institutions and their relations with individual countries, companies, governments, and each other. Commercial banks, to take only the most obvious example, are more different one from another than outsiders might (and do) believe. They exist in a number of different institutional and legal settings which give them different obligations and opportunities. They have different sorts of shareholders, and are subjected to wide and differing ranges of public pressures. Their behaviour can often be a reflection of the legal, political and social environment they have to do business in, rather than the personal preferences of their senior managers and/or boards of directors. They are also bureaucratic institutions, with rules, methods and principles guiding their paths of action. Some of them are centres of intellectual excellence, where a great deal of hard research and thinking is done.

Anyone who tries to look objectively at the political economy of apartheid, and at the international institutions of finance that have had dealings with its agents, must start from the unglamorous and often neglected position that the world is a complex place, and that the first part of analysis lies in trying to understand it. This is our first concern in this book.

Our second concern is more practical. In common with other people of goodwill throughout the world, right across the political spectrum, we wish to see apartheid brought to an end, and replaced with a democratic system that is responsive to all the citizens of South Africa. Our reasons for this, and for believing that it is a feasible project, in so far as these reasons touch on the political economy of South Africa, are set out in chapter two. Here we also address the fact that white South Africans and their supporters elsewhere in the world often point out that there are many societies which do not practise democracy. They ask why they should be singled out for criticism and 'interference'. The question is a fair one and deserves an answer.

In chapter three we sketch, more or less without comment, what seem to us to be the main features of recent developments in the South African economy. Our focus is not on the moral dimension of the policy of apartheid, which is widely understood, though we wish it to be known that we share the humanitarian revulsion for it which is surely the natural response of any civilised person. Our focus is, rather, through the usual conceptual apparatus of the discipline of economics, the current state of the South African economy: the macroeconomic stance that its policy-makers are taking; the economic pressures that are weighing on the domestic South African economy from the international economy; and the accumulated effects of forty years of apartheid on such matters as the allocation of resources, the shape of the labour market, and the capacity for structural adjustment at a time of rapid change in the world economy as a whole. In our view there has been too little 'positive' economic analysis of apartheid (though we are conscious that this situation of neglect is changing in South Africa itself). We believe such analysis can make a contribution to critical understanding.

Together these two chapters constitute Part I of the book.

Part II is an empirical and descriptive account of South Africa's present relations with the world of international finance. In chapter four we trace the course of the foreign debt crisis that broke in 1985, forcing the Republic to default on its international debt obligations. We describe the process by which the interim agreements between South Africa and its creditors were reached, and explain the details of these agreements – the commitments that have been made and how they are fulfilled. We give as much information as we can about the prospects for the new debt rescheduling negotiations which are to occur before June 1990, and explain why the debt problem continues to be a source of grave anxiety in policy-making circles in Pretoria.

In chapter five we set out the principal lines of the policy that the South African government has sought to pursue since 1985 in order to stabilise its capital account and regain admission to world capital markets. In particular we give a detailed description of the dual exchange rate system: both of how it works and of what its effects are.

This analysis is augmented in chapter six by a brisk and non-technical treatment of the underlying problems that South Africa confronts with capital flows: the prospects for future medium- and long-term loans; the trade credit system and how it works; and the process of disinvestment by foreign companies. This last phenomenon has been accelerating over the past three years, and we attempt to assess what impact it is having, and on whom.

Chapter seven is devoted to gold.

This is not yet another book about trade sanctions against South Africa. For what it is worth, however, we believe that the anti-apartheid movement outside South Africa may risk becoming isolated from the evolution of debate and analysis in the anti-apartheid movement inside South Africa about the utility of blanket sanctions as an instrument in the process of exerting pressure for change. We have to discuss gold, however, because it occupies a special position in the economy of South Africa as both a tradeable commodity, with industrial and commercial uses, and as a currency in international exchange. Its central role as a linchpin of the whole economy is elaborated and analysed. The thesis that we develop, that South African gold is of increasing insignificance in the world economy, and its capacity to sustain the economy of apartheid inside South Africa progressively diminishing as a result, may come as a surprise. The impact of these developments, if we are right, is very great, however, and provides a springboard to the third and final part of the book.

How international financial institutions are now, and can in the future, play a part in the transformation of South Africa from a closed racist oligarchy to an open, multi-racial democracy, is the dominant theme of chapter eight. Here we set out some proposals on policies for the financial sector in Western countries that could be expected to hasten the collapse of apartheid under conditions conducive to a negotiated, rather than a bloody, settlement. Then we attempt briefly to draw all of these threads together to show that there is still a route open that can produce effective change in South Africa, and that can do so in the relatively short term.

The thrust of this book is policy oriented, and there are some reasons for this which it is appropriate that we should explain.

A part of our work owes its origins to the political life of the Commonwealth of Nations. The South African government, with its policy of apartheid, has posed both a problem and a challenge to the Commonwealth throughout its entire existence. The course of the bad relations has been neither steady nor unidirectional, however. The rhythm of disaffection and discord has fluctuated according to developments inside South Africa itself.

After Sharpeville, and the tightening of oppression in 1960, South Africa was compelled, by its own intransigence, to leave the Commonwealth in 1961. As the full repressive implications of apartheid became increasingly evident throughout the 1960s, the Commonwealth played a significant role in helping to secure international agreement on banning the sale of arms to South Africa. It has also played some role in securing the subsequent restrictions, such as they are, on the sale to South Africa of computer technology, oil, and nuclear services and equipment.

After the traumatic explosions of black urban unrest in the South African winter of 1976, a period of violence which happened to coincide with a long tour of South Africa by the New Zealand Rugby Football Union's national team, the Commonwealth played the leading role, through what became known as the Gleneagles Agreement, in isolating most of South African team sport from competition with the rest of the world.

During and after the renewed outbreaks of turmoil in 1985 and 1986, Commonwealth leaders once again found that the issue of South Africa could not be kept away from the top of its agenda. At their regular two-yearly meeting in October 1985, held at Nassau in the Bahamas, Commonwealth heads of government drew up an accord on southern Africa that reaffirmed their commitment to the trade and sporting measures of earlier years, and agreed a process for the creation and funding of what was to become known as the Eminent Persons Group (EPG).

The group consisted of seven eminent Commonwealth citizens drawn from the five continents and combining a wealth of experience in many diverse fields. The group was jointly chaired by Malcolm Fraser, the former Prime Minister of Australia (1975–83) and by General Olusegun Obasanjo, the former head of the Federal Military Government of Nigeria (1976-79). Their brief was 'to encourage through all practicable ways the evolution of [the] necessary process of political dialogue' as part of a concerted attempt to bring about the dismantling of apartheid and the creation of 'structures of democracy' in South Africa.

The story of the EPG's odyssey in South Africa is told superbly well in their own report (Commonwealth Group of Eminent Persons 1986). In the first half of 1986 briefly, and miraculously, it seemed for a while to the outside world that they might actually succeed: that the various leaders of the different communities might actually be prepared to accept a 'negotiating concept', commit their supporters to a cessation of all violence, and agree to sit down to find a human solution to their now almost inhuman problems.

It was surely the real possibility of success being within reach that made all the more dispiriting the South African government's regrettably brutal repudiation of the EPG's 'negotiating concept'. Showing the disregard for international law which has been a constant accompaniment to the South African regime's insistence that her own system of law should not be interfered in by outsiders, the South African Defence Force launched military attacks on African National Congress 'bases' in Botswana, Zambia and Zimbabwe on 19 May, the very day that the EPG was to hold a meeting with the members of the South African Cabinet Constitutional Committee to discuss the possible acceptance of their proposals. The regime could hardly have spoken more eloquently.

The members of the EPG believed, and reported, that their efforts had resulted in failure. With hindsight we believe that this judgement, though correct in the sense that radical political transformation did not flow directly from the process of dialogue which they initiated, might now be seen as too modest and perhaps over-reactive.

For one thing, South African political opinion has not been the same since the EPG exercise. There is now apparent in South Africa, for the first time in forty years, a fairly widespread assumption about the need for change, and also a very great deal of thinking about how it might be accomplished. We think some of the credit for this transformation of attitudes lies with the remarkable journey, moral and intellectual as well as physical, that was made by the members of the Eminent Persons Group.

Secondly, in early August 1986 those Commonwealth heads of government who had been charged by the meeting in Nassau with defining the modalities of the EPG exercise (the President of Zambia, and the Prime Ministers of Australia, the Bahamas, Canada, India, the United Kingdom and Zimbabwe) held a review meeting with the members of the EPG to consider what might be done next.

This London meeting accepted that the EPG exercise had failed, but proposed that its main contribution – that the leaders of all communities in South Africa collectively negotiate, without violence, a democratic solution to the country's problems – should lie on the table. With the dissenting voice of Britain, they also agreed on the implementation of a series of further sanctions and pressures on the white regime in South Africa that had been foreshadowed at Nassau ten months earlier.

The Commonwealth's commitment to the negotiating concept was reaffirmed a year later in the statement and program of action on southern Africa prepared by the Commonwealth heads of government at their meeting at Lake Okanagan, near Vancouver, in mid-October 1987. Once again, Commonwealth leaders could see that it was not simply a question of how to persuade the National Party government in South Africa to go to the negotiating table, but of how to apply pressure to convince it of the need to do so. With this objective in mind, though once again with the regrettable exception of Britain, whose Prime Minister did not agree with the proposal, the heads of government agreed: 'given the significance of South Africa's relationship with the international financial system and the need for a better understanding of developments and possibilities in this sphere [to] initiate an expert study, drawing on independent sources, to examine this aspect of the South African economy'. The original suggestion for this initiative was put forward at the meeting by the Prime Minister of Australia, Mr Bob Hawke.

In tandem with this decision, and again with the exception of Britain, the heads of government also agreed to set up a Committee of Foreign Ministers 'able to meet periodically to provide high level impetus and guidance' in furtherance of the quest for a resolution of the problem of South Africa. They agreed to appoint to this committee the foreign ministers of Australia, Canada, Guyana, India, Nigeria, Tanzania, Zambia and Zimbabwe, with Canada to be in the chair.

The Commonwealth Foreign Ministers' Committee on Southern Africa (CFMSA), set up by the Okanagan statement, held its first meeting in the Zambian capital of Lusaka in the first week of February 1988. At this meeting the ministers agreed to give substance to the proposal for a study of South Africa's international financial links by appointing a committee of experts to study the subject and, drawing on outside expertise, to report within nine months. Australia, Canada and India agreed to participate in the work and, through the co-ordinating offices of the Commonwealth Secretariat, set up a five-person officials' committee to undertake the research. The five members of this committee were Tony Cole, who acted as chairman, and Terry O'Brien from the public service in Australia, Anthony Burger and Bethany Armstrong from the public service in Canada, and K. L. Deshpande, from the Reserve Bank of India. In addition to the research services that it was able to secure from participating governments, the committee received considerable assistance and guidance from the international financial community who, for the most part, were prepared to speak frankly off the record. The committee submitted its report, titled *South Africa's Relationship with the International Financial System*, to the second meeting of CFMSA, which met in Toronto, Canada, at the beginning of August 1988.

The report contained a number of original insights, but perhaps its biggest impact derived from the fact that it uncovered a field of activity linking apartheid to the rest of the world that had not been much considered in the international community. The foreign ministers believed that it would be appropriate to try to draw it to the attention of a larger audience.

To this end, the Australian Minister for Foreign Affairs and Trade, Senator Gareth Evans, proposed at the third meeting of the CFMSA, held in Harare in early February 1989, that his government would undertake to bring what had by this time become known colloquially as 'The Financial Links Study' up to date, by analysing the developments of 1988-89; adding some new material on the political consequences of the relationship between international finance and the apartheid regime; rewriting the somewhat technical report in a way that would make it more accessible to a larger audience; and having it published. The original report itself is to be made available by the Commonwealth Secretariat, which is arranging to have it published verbatim by James Currey.

This book is the product of the offer made by the Australian Minister for Foreign Affairs and Trade. We have told of its origins in some detail here because we are concerned that the status of our work should be understood. *Apartheid and International Finance: A Program for Change* lies in direct line of descent from the Eminent Persons Group's *Mission to Africa*, and is to be interpreted in the light of the Commonwealth's commitment to the pursuit of peaceful change. It is, however, our book. Though its origins lie in the work of an officials' committee, and its publication has been made possible by the Australian federal government, we have been left completely free to conduct our analysis, interpret our findings, and express our preferences without political interference of any kind. The book contains our joint, personal convictions. Naturally we hope that they will convince others, including those with the weighty responsibilities of state to attend to.

Keith Ovenden was invited to join the project shortly after the Australian minister's offer had been accepted by his Commonwealth colleagues, and he is primarily responsible for all the bridging work that has turned 'The Financial Links Study' into this book. He conducted a full round of new interviews with members of the international financial community, and he is first author of all the material contained in chapters one, two and eight. He is also primarily responsible for bringing the material in chapters three to seven up to date, reorganising and in some considerable degree extending it, and putting it into rather less technical language. It is our joint hope that readers with no background in economics will be able to follow the argument without difficulty throughout, but if this is not so, whatever responsibility for the failure that can be said to lie with the authors lies most with him.

Despite these caveats, the book remains a truly collaborative work. Both authors are conscious of the contribution that was made by the other four members of the original committee, and in particular by Terry O'Brien, who has made a substantial research contribution to this rather larger and somewhat different work.

Keith Ovenden is particularly keen to record his gratitude to Tony Cole, who generously accommodated him to a project that was already a year old when he joined. Tony has been an ideal partner in the business of writing, a role that has been in addition to his normal duties as a senior officer in the Australian Department of Prime Minister and Cabinet. Both of us are also very conscious of the co-operative pleasure that we have taken in each other's fields of expertise. George Orwell was fond of saying that no one would write a book if he or she knew in advance the self-inflicted pain that the process of doing so would cause. We think there is a lot of pleasure too, and even, despite the bleakness of the topic and the horrors that apartheid both embraces and conceals, a lot of personal enrichment.

We think it is fair to say that, generally speaking, intellectual life in the West is not much influenced by politics. The same cannot be said of the reverse. Political discourse, though there are lags, is profoundly influenced by the worlds of ideas, research and analysis. It is perhaps what sometimes gives to academics and intellectuals the overdeveloped sense of their own political omniscience which is one of the less lovely characteristics of university life.

In this instance we are happy to record a simple truth: that the book, and whatever claims to intellectual rigour might reasonably be made on its behalf, have come directly from the political initiatives of public people grappling with a shared and very public problem. But for the collective and individual actions of politicians this book would never have been written. In this regard we particularly wish to record our gratitude to Senator Evans, and his Commonwealth foreign minister colleagues, for giving us this opportunity to try to make a constructive contribution to what we hope can be a peaceful resolution of one of the most evil and intractable problems of our age.

Part I

CHAPTER TWO

Why South Africa Is Different

Everyone knows what is wrong with South Africa. Its government is illegitimate because it rests on the systematic institutionalisation of racism. This racism would be unacceptable to the rest of the world even if it were founded on the consent of the majority of the governed. But it is not. Instead it is derived from a morally and intellectually discredited theory that is employed to justify the exclusive exercise of power by whites over all other races.

The black people, 75% of the population, do not have the right to vote in any national elections; are not permitted to participate in many of the principal political organisations of their choice; are deprived of most of their leaders, who are either in prison or in exile; and are robbed of their civil liberties to a degree that would be considered intolerable in all Western democratic societies. That these same conditions also apply, in some if not exactly the same degree, to the members of o ler non-white races, and to those whites who actively oppose apartheid policies, emphasises the illegitimacy of the regime. Consent is not a priority. Coercion comes first.

The government of South Africa knows that it has a problem of legitimacy. In an attempt to dispel it, the regime has adopted a policy of forcing black people to live in the so-called homelands, or Bantustans, the approximately 13% of the land area of the Republic that has been set aside for black people to govern and administer their own affairs. Four of them, Transkei, Bophuthatswana, Venda and Ciskei (TBVC) have been given a spurious and unrecognised independence, while the remainder are currently still a part of the Republic of South Africa. The homelands serve a number of purposes, chief among which is social control of the population in defence of white economic interests. However the homelands are also an instrument of constitutional control, enabling the white regime to claim that black South Africans, not being citizens of the Republic of South Africa, do not have any political rights there. Instead they hold them in their homelands. The black populations of these 'states' (both those that are independent already, and those that are to become so) have not, by this logic, been disenfranchised in South Africa because they are not entitled to vote there in the first place. They are foreigners – foreigners in their own country.

The constitutional implications of this are more far reaching than may be commonly understood. For instance, the abolition of the Pass Laws in 1986 has generally been presented to the world at large as evidence of the serious resolve of the white regime to carry out meaningful reform. The reality is that although repeal of the Pass Laws has marginally lightened the burden of many (and has certainly set in train dynamic economic developments that may well fracture the whole structure of apartheid), it has also worsened the position of about a third of the black population. These are the people who are deemed to be citizens of one or other of the four independent homelands, and who may now be subject to immigration laws under which they may be 'expelled' from their place of residence or work without any right of appeal. Promises made in 1975 (Leach 1986, 86) that this situation would not be allowed to develop, have never been kept. Most of the black population of Cape Town, who as Xhosa-speakers are regarded by the regime as citizens of either Ciskei or Transkei, now live under this threat (Wilson & Ramphele 1989, 212). It places them on a footing of unhappy equality with the nationals of Mozambique, Lesotho, Botswana, Swaziland and elsewhere, who make up South Africa's substantial migrant labour force.

It is clear to anyone who has studied it that the homelands policy is a fraud, with no justification in history, anthropology or political thought (Keppel-Jones 1968; Thompson 1985), but by inventing and imposing it, the white settlers of South Africa have created a formidable impediment both to reform and to economic development. Development is essentially a history of urbanisation and the creation of domestic markets – large aggregations of purchasing power. Apartheid, in some of its facets, seems to be an attempt to prevent this from happening.

That they have a sense that reform is required, however, is illustrated by the attempts at constitutional adjustment that have been undertaken in the past ten years. The most significant of these has been the Republic of South Africa Constitution Act, which was signed into law in September 1983, and subsequently endorsed by a referendum of the white population on 2 November of the same year.

The process by which this legislation was adopted began in June 1980 with the passage of the Republic of South Africa Constitution Fifth Amendment Bill which abolished the old upper chamber, the Senate, and created (though not in its place) a President's Council of sixty white, coloured (including one Chinese) and Indian people appointed by the President to make recommendations for a new constitution that would take account of the coloured and Indian populations.

The President's Council reported in May 1982, and proposed the creation of a new executive presidency by merging the functions of Prime Minister and State President (then a more or less purely ceremonial office). The presidency was to provide strong executive power, and was to have only an indirect relationship with even the minority electorate, since it was not to be filled by popular election but by an electoral college chosen by and from the legislature. The structure of the new legislature was not defined by the council, although they recommended that it have white, coloured and Indian members.

The government produced its own draft proposals for a new constitution a year later, in May 1983. These proposals were subsequently embodied in the Republic of South Africa Constitution Bill that began its journey through parliament two months later. The legislation, as passed, created a tricameral parliament with a House of Assembly for whites with, as before, 178 members; a House of Representatives for coloureds with 85 members; and a House of Delegates for Indians with 45 members. The chambers have members in proportion, very roughly, of 4:2:1 (matching their numbers in the non-black society generally), but these proportions are entrenched in the legislation, so that they may not be changed even when or if the proportionate sizes of the various communities change.

Each house of parliament formally has control over its 'Own Affairs', which include social welfare, education, health, housing and local government issues. And each has its own Ministers' Council as an executive arm to implement and administer decisions.

In practice the power of coloured and Indian houses over their 'Own Affairs' is considerably constrained. 'General Affairs', which include finance, defence, foreign affairs, justice, transport, commerce and industry, all ultimately come under white parliamentary control. At the margins, when there are matters of dispute over what is or is not an 'Own Affair' as opposed to a 'General Affair', it is the State President who decides.

The President is elected by an electoral college chosen by and from the three houses of parliament in the same 4:2:1 proportions, and he holds office for the life of the parliament. He appoints the Cabinet, presides over its deliberations, and has the power to declare war and a state of martial law.

One prominent writer about contemporary South African affairs (Lipton 1988) refers to these reforms as 'bizarre'. They certainly are. The fact that the races are kept artificially apart in separate chambers (though there is a system of committees for them to 'harmonise' their decisions); the relative sizes of the chambers; the extraction of financial control (though each does have its own budget), justice, commerce and industry, and transport from the field of 'Own Affairs'; and the method of election of the President: all are designed to ensure white domination. Just in case the other races were not prepared to accept constitutional domination of this kind, whites were permitted to vote in a referendum on whether they approved of the reform or not, but coloureds and Indians were offered no such opportunity.

Small wonder that most opponents of apartheid inside South Africa regarded the constitutional reform as a cosmetic non-sense. In the first elections to the new chambers, held on 22 August 1984 for Coloureds and 29 August for Indians, the turnout was, respectively, 30% and 20%.

We have dwelt on the details of these constitutional changes for three reasons:

(a) because they illustrate that the regime is uncomfortably aware of its illegitimacy and that it would like to do something about it if it could do so without fundamentally disturbing the status quo.

(b) because it illustrates one subsidiary theme of our approach: that there is a process of rethinking going on inside South Africa and, limited as its results have thus far been, they do show signs, as most thinking will eventually, of having to face the real issues. (Lipton 1987 contains further details on government reform proposals.)

(c) because in a direct and interesting way the reforms illustrate our central thesis: that apartheid involves the systematic misallocation of resources and the introduction of burdensome structural imbalances in the economy.

In the financial year 1985–86, as a direct consequence of the introduction of the tricameral system of central government administration, budget expenditure on central government rose by slightly more than 108% over the previous year! The following year it rose by another 72%. Estimates for 1987–88 involved a further increase of 12.5%. Central administration in South Africa now accounts for 8.5 billion Rand of the total 1988–89 budget of just under 54 billion Rand, or nearly a sixth of all central government expenditure.

It would be hard to sustain the argument that South African citizens, the vast majority of whom – coloured, Indian and black – have not voted for the strange system of pseudo-democracy through which they are now ruled, are getting value for money. Waste is one characteristic of autocracies, so perhaps we should not be surprised. The constitutional example helps to illustrate, however, an argument that will recur: that in economic and financial terms, the people of South Africa pay a very high price for apartheid (Savage 1986, *passim*).

Another feature of this cosmetic constitutional reform, with the misallocation of resources that it entails, is that it should have come at exactly the time when virtually all of the developed democracies of the Western world are pruning central administrations and deregulating their economies. The worldwide movement (it is more than a tendency) is towards recognition of the need for far more managerial professionalism in central government, and for far greater harmonisation of domestic arrangements in order to facilitate transfers – of labour, capital, technology, information, and so on – in a shrinking world.

While most of the rest of the world is seeking to get the best out of all its people by stripping away regulatory and other impediments to individual initiative and accomplishment, South Africa is spending more on elaborate machinery and repression to maintain socio-economic rankings based on race rather than achievement. Because of this apartheid is of legitimate interest and concern to the West, and the more that the South African regime persists with its various policy positions, so it will progressively become of more interest. Moreover, it is perverse of white South Africans to complain that this should be so, for it is something which they are doing to themselves.

Despite the self-evident nature of this proposition, many white South Africans persist in believing that it is not the substance but the appearance of apartheid and its affects that matters on the world stage. They seem to believe that in the world of constitutional politics, as in the worlds of show business or soap powder marketing, presentation is all.

At one level perhaps there is a dismal though trivial truth in this. If television film of black people being shot on the streets of Soweto can be kept from the American public, demands for an alteration in policy from the United States federal administration may be expected to diminish. Certainly lobbyists in the United States are conscious of how much harder it has become to put the anti-apartheid case there since media censorship was introduced in South Africa under the state of emergency. None the less, constitutional matters do not disappear when the floodlights are turned away from them. The heart of South Africa's dilemma is that it has systematically constructed, for reasons of ideology, a system of government that deprives more than three-quarters of its citizens of control over their circumstances by excluding them from the political arena. This fact is now so well understood in the Western world that it cannot be ignored by any politician.

Communication plays an essential element in this. It is true that the regime can keep today's pictures of its brutality from the dinner tables of the affluent West, but it cannot suppress more than a fraction of the exchange of information that has arisen as a result of the worldwide expansion in communication that has occurred over the past fifteen years (Lipton 1985, 413). Inside the Republic itself there has been a renewed upsurge of criticism of the regime, much of it from the business community, from a newly invigorated opposition (white as well as black), and even from within the government's own ranks. Outside South Africa the amount of information now in circulation, its quality, and the standards of research that are being committed, all mean that South Africa can no longer rely on neglect born of ignorance for safety from the critical reactions of the West. Apartheid cannot hide because it has become public property. It is useful to reflect on the reasons for this because they illustrate one underlying theme which informs some of our argument in this book.

History shows that economic change transforms societies.

With growth, capital accumulation, industrial development and rising living standards, comes the evolution of social structure. New social classes emerge, old ones disintegrate or decay. The new emerging social structure gives birth to new institutions that reflect the concerns and preoccupations of people as economic developments exercise their weight upon them. Industrialising societies breed mass publics distributed around cleavages of class, status and race. Their concerns are with conflict at the workplace – union versus employer; with the pursuit of greater social justice – wealthy versus the poor; and with matters of welfare, health and education – the transfer of resources from private consumption towards collective security through the service and 'humane' industries.

Industrial society produces political movements and parties that articulate the various sides of these conflicts. Out of their resolution – because the vast majority of conflicts are resolved, one way or another – grow the institutions of law, representation and public administration that are in turn the great arenas of decision-making in the political lives of industrial society.

Any country that adopts, whether by design or as a consequence of unwilled forces, the path of industrial development, will experience social effects of this kind. They will vary according to the character of the local pre-industrial culture and its tenacity in a setting of increasing industrialisation; according to whether the industrial development is patchy or uniform in its impact; and according to the sequence of types of production that occurs. However, in broad outline, economic development leads to a particular outcome which we call industrial society.

There is much evidence now to suggest that in the wake of industrialisation there flows another current of development, one that is commonly referred to as post-industrial, and which itself generates a further transformation of the social structure in the societies where it occurs. Under the pressures of structural adjustment, as old industries die and new high-technology industries are born, the structure of society is again redefined. The effect is to squeeze the old institutions that had previously articulated demands, to break the old alliances, and to focus attention on newly defined problems, many of them the direct consequence of the growth of technology itself (Apter 1971; Bell 1973; Boulding 1978; Touraine 1971).

It is a commonplace that the current evolution of society in its post-industrial form is difficult to understand, easy to misinterpret, and hard to forecast. What is generally believed to be true, however, is that where the process of transformation from pre-industrial to industrial society is overtaken by the growth of post-industrial conditions before it is itself largely complete, then the consequent effects on social structure are of great complexity. (For two different views of complexity see Giddens 1973; La Porte 1975.)

We take the view that this is what is happening in South Africa, and that view informs the way we have approached our subject. We argue that what happens on the economic front is what gives preponderant weight to developments on the sometimes more visible fronts of social movements, political conflicts and public ideologies. This is not to say that the social movements, political conflicts and ideological struggles are in any way less important. On the contrary, by far the most important question about South Africa today is: can this troubled society manage to get from repressive apartheid to some sort of constitutional settlement in which the primary commitment is to the exercise of the democratic method, without the disaster of a bloody civil war which would ruin the prospects for liberty and wreck the economic structures on which growth and security for the future depend?

In the context of this question it should be recognised that as a result of the sort of industrial and political development that they have experienced, South Africans are no longer in a position fully to control what happens in their society. It has long been an axiom of economic thought that many people each pursuing his or her own perceived self-interest may, through their collective interaction, generate outcomes that none of them individually wants. South Africa has clearly entered a phase of its history in which this axiom can be seen to be at work in its politics.

How could South Africa not, in these circumstances, attract the interest of the outside world? The evolution of its affairs has an almost hypnotic fascination for anyone concerned for social development and the problems of world order. In particular, no government of a major power can afford not to take a close and active interest in what is happening there, because of its effects on both the rest of Africa and international relations generally.

Alongside the *post hoc* attempts at constitutional reform in South Africa, designed to camouflage from scrutiny the problem of democratic legitimacy, has flourished an argument of pseudo-anthropology that has long been one of apartheid's attempted justifications of racism: an article of faith in its ideological constellation. In brief, this argument holds that black people are, through nature and history, less mature, intelligent and competent than white people. Their willing consent to the prevailing political arrangements is not necessary, according to this proposition, because black people lack the necessary gifts of maturity and competence to be entrusted with government.

Assertions of this kind have a long and dismal lineage (Gould 1981), though no substance either in fact or in social theory. In South Africa, however, they have survived in an institutionalised way in defence of political illegitimacy. Government here, the argument runs, cannot be by the consent of the majority because the majority is not capable of according its consent in a way that is commensurate with the obligations that flow from citizenship in a democracy. This argument shows how little democratic theory is understood by proponents of the apartheid regime. There is a long and persuasive literature to show that it is never good practice, as a matter of prudence as well as a matter of principle, to recommend that others be deprived of rights and obligations that you find necessary and congenial in the exercise of your own liberty (Lucas 1976). There is persuasive evidence from recent empirical democratic theory to show that the democratic method is more efficient, more responsive and more 'intelligent' than alternative forms of government (Barry 1965).

There is some evidence to show that some white South Africans are coming to understand the force of these arguments, and are anxious to find a way out of the labyrinth of deception, fear and violence in which they have become trapped by the empty political and social theory of apartheid.

Others, however, particularly on the right wing of the National Party; in the breakaway Conservative Party; in the neo-Nazi Afrikaner Weerstandsbeweging (Afrikaner Resistance Movement) and its militant uniformed paramilitary organisation the Boerevag (Boer Guard); and in the Volkswag (People's Guard), an umbrella group led by Voerwoerd's son-in-law, Carel Boshoff, that claims to be non-political, remain convinced that racial theories can explain and justify social relations. In them, however, '[t]he nostalgia for the past, evident in the terminology of dissent, and the hankering after a secure Afrikaner homeland, amount to an admission of defeat' (Uys 1987, 68).

Orthodox National Party opinion is now less preoccupied by theoretical matters. Its concern is power: power over the land, over the economy, over the people. The party's members have a mythology to account for and justify their proprietorship of power, and their view of the outside world is highly coloured by the belief that the land being theirs, they should be left alone to do with it (and its inhabitants) what they wish. To their way of thinking there are plenty of countries that have governments that do not rule by consent, so why pick on South Africa as a special case?

This is a difficult question for people in the West to understand, partly because the answers to it seem so obvious, and partly because the asking of it has always suggested that there was a problem of discourse with white South Africa: that we were not speaking the same language, or at any rate not employing the same concepts, so dialogue was stunted and deformed. The answers to it touch closely, however, on the broad field of the South African economy, and the nature of its relations with international finance, so it is appropriate to give at least a brief account of the answer here in order to clear the ground for what is to follow.

For a start it is hardly true that the West has picked on South Africa. For fully thirteen years after the National Party first came to power in 1948 South Africa continued to be a full member, in good standing, of the Western community, including the multiracial Commonwealth of Nations. How white South Africans might honestly have expected to be able to continue to belong to that body once the black regimes of Africa and the Caribbean had begun to take their rightful places at the table is hard to imagine. Certainly from any viewpoint of rationality such an expectation seems peculiar. Nevertheless, it took the horror of the Sharpeville shootings of 1960 to provoke action by member countries to expel South Africa from the Commonwealth. South Africa withdrew in 1961 to pre-empt its certain expulsion.

Even after 1961, however, the West practised a cautious, even collusive patience with South Africa. Despite the continued application of increasingly rigorous measures of coercive control, the West did little to disown apartheid. Military co-ordination and assistance continued throughout the sixties. Sporting contacts remained virtually normal until 1970. Meaningful sanctions, that is ones that were selected for having a reasonable chance of success, and were supported by a sufficiently large number of advanced countries, did not become a prominent part of the West's practical expression of disillusionment with the apartheid regime for more than a decade after that.

Any reasonable response to the question 'Why pick on South Africa?' must surely begin from the admission that Western countries have been astonishingly tolerant of apartheid, and that it is a wonder that this tolerance still has not expired in some influential quarters.

Part of the explanation for this relatively long history of tolerance of apartheid lies in questions of strategic security. It became an axiomatic part of the West's analysis of cold war strategy (especially with the closure of the Suez Canal in 1956) that the trade routes around the Cape demanded an alliance with South Africa, no matter what its internal politics. Whether there was ever much truth in this position, which we doubt, the current fact is that the world has changed. Cold war considerations of this kind are no longer of such critical importance, and Western defence interests involve new and different strategies. This does not mean that South Africa is no longer of any strategic interest to the West, however. Rather, it means that there is a far clearer recognition in the West that its interest lies in having a strong and developing South Africa as part of the community of democratic nations.

This is yet another reason why, forty years after the ideologues of apartheid came to power, Western nations are showing signs of having run out of patience. For instance, only twenty-five years ago South Africa was able to enter into collusion with the French governments of Charles de Gaulle and Georges Pompidou to manipulate the world gold market. One result of this alliance of interests was that it led in 1971 (though it was far from being the only cause) to the abandoning of a fixed price for gold, the devaluation of the US dollar, and the ushering in of a decade of disorder in world currency markets (Johnson 1977, 70–82).

Today, far from being able to forge a similar alliance of self-interest with France, South Africa finds itself confronted with bi-partisan condemnation from Paris. The fact that the 1977 world embargo on arms sales to South Africa was supported by the French administration of President Giscard d'Estaing came as a surprise to South Africa. (France had not complied with the 1963 voluntary arms embargo, and had been the major supplier of high-technology military equipment to South Africa for a decade after that.) The EEC sanctions of the mid-1980s (finance, computers, iron and steel, coal, oil) were introduced under the socialist administration of President Mitterrand and Prime Minister Laurent Fabius. Fabius was also instrumental in imposing a ban on new French investments in South Africa. When Jacques Chirac, of the RPR (Gaullist) coalition became Prime Minister in 1986 he did not alter the French stance on sanctions (though he did reinstate the French ambassador in South Africa), and there are signs of further hardening in the French Position since Michel Rocard became Prime Minister and the Socialists returned to office after the elections of May and June 1988.

To give another example: only a dozen years ago it was confidently asserted by some South Africa watchers that the United States would be unlikely to act firmly on the issue of apartheid until compelled to do so by cold war considerations (Johnson 1977, 322). In the event, exactly the opposite has been the case. The cold war has ebbed away, and with (though not solely because of) its decline has come a sharply augmented American hostility to apartheid. In 1986 Congress passed, and President Reagan signed into law, the Comprehensive Anti-Apartheid Act (CAAA) which, among many other things, prohibits United States banks from making loans available to most South African entities. Only loans that can be shown to be for the development of black enterprise and opportunity are exempt. American companies with investments in South Africa could keep them, but were not permitted further investment. A year later, a new provision required American companies to pay US federal taxes as well as South African taxes on profits from their South African operations. Disinvestment by American companies, partly as a result of these measures (which we discuss in more detail in chapter six) is now a major feature of American-South African relations.

To add emphasis to these two illustrations of how South Africa's relations with the rest of the world have been changing faster than seemed possible a few years ago, a delegation of ANC leaders to Moscow in early March 1989 was told that the Soviet Union 'would prefer a political settlement and want apartheid to be dealt with by political means'. The head of the Soviet Union's Foreign Ministry Department of African Countries, Yuri Yukalov, was reported as saying that 'South Africa should not be destroyed . . . There should be dialogue'. Later the same month the Soviet Union was host to joint talks between the ANC and two prominent members of the anti-apartheid movement in South Africa, Alex Boraine and Frederik van Zyl Slabbert of the Institute for a Democratic Alternative in South Africa (IDASA) (*Age, Australian,* 17 March 1989). These developments suggest a new though still emerging world consensus on the sorts of pressures that are likely to help generate change in South Africa.

In our view, the reasons for this have to do with the evolution of the advanced economies, just as the transformation of the political and social situation in South Africa is itself a product of economic developments there. The rapid shift towards post-industrial conditions in the advanced countries is far from complete and still extremely difficult to analyse, but some patterns can be fairly readily detected. One is a shift in political interest among the new emerging professional and technical classes from issues of narrow personal self-interest to those of value and broad ethical concern. Modernity in Apter's terminology (Apter 1971) is characterised by an acute concern for issues of principle in the context of theoretical orientations towards social objects. Modern politics are increasingly driven, in the developed economies of both East and West, by the growing class of 'theory' workers, the expanding labour force of the new high technology and service industries. Their interests are ones of flexible personal freedoms, expanded personal liberty, and abstract, even symbolic issues of value, such as the pursuit of justice in fields like racial and gender equality. The authoritarian working class (Lipset 1981) is in decay throughout the developed world, not just among white South Africans but more rapidly still in the advanced developed countries.

These changes, which we have sketched very lightly, help to explain the widespread and increasing condemnation of South Africa. The regime's reliance on a doctrine of racial separation which, in practice, has also come to mean repression, is progressively out of harmony with the political values that are being generated in response to the economic transformation of industrial into post-industrial society.

There is a cultural force at work here too. Since the military destruction of German fascism, the Western reaction to doctrines of racial oppression and of genocide has evolved and matured. The history of the mass graves of central Europe and the labour camps of the Gulag Archipelago haunt the imaginations and the minds of educated Western men and women. Racism and coercive repression have become more unacceptable to civilisation as our historical knowledge of them has deepened.

The discovery by a new generation of mass, educated publics in the Western world of the deep-seated nature of racism in the colonial past of their own eighteenth- and nineteenth-century forebears, has stimulated a re-evaluation of history.

The practice of racism in the age of Steiner, Arendt, Primo Levi and Kundera is now widely perceived as a regression into ethical bankruptcy. As Steiner has said, there is no statement competent to embrace the full moral dimension of the horror that our immediate forebears have committed (Steiner 1971).

South Africans are currently keen to tell the West that their attitudes are changing and that they should be given time. It is no disservice to tell them, in return, that attitudes in the West have been changing too, and that time – which is another way of describing further long years of illegitimate and repressive government – is not something, in the field of race relations, of which there is an oversupply.

If advocates of the South African regime really wish to know why the West is losing patience with its political and social practices, much of the answer may lie in the rapidly changing sociology of the West. The sense of the need and propriety of liberal freedoms for all people has been growing quickly, and it has been coupled with the growing perception of the world as a single, unified entity, bound together by its problems as much as by its promise. In this context the racism of apartheid makes of the regime a special case, and one that requires special treatment.

It is commonly argued, not least by white South Africans,

that there are other countries that practise racism, and these countries are not singled out for particular attention. Strictly as a matter of fact this is not so. Distinguishing first between the institutional framework of law in the Western countries and actual practices in those societies, there is not one of either the OECD nations or the forty-eight member countries of the Commonwealth that has a constitution or a system of public institutions that enshrines the unequal treatment of citizens on the basis of race.

Of course it is true that racist behaviour occurs in many, probably all, modern societies, and that the causes of it are deep-rooted and persistent. The civil rights records of almost all Western countries are far from unblemished under scrutiny. But they can be scrutinised. And there are generally legal remedies available to rectify injustices. Above all, ordinary people in advanced Western industrialised societies are free to engage in political organisations that may offer them opportunities to effect reform, and to regulate the processes in society which they themselves detect as harmful to their interests. We do not try to pretend that there are not political and social problems in Western countries. What we do argue is that the democratic method is efficient at identifying problems and at releasing energies for their solution.

In this sense societies that are governed without consent have a double problem: they must contain the demands of those whom they oppress without ever being able fully to know what their demands are, or what would satisfy their aspirations. The organised racism of present-day apartheid is, in this sense, a modern-day equivalent of all the old European political forces which, in the eighteenth and nineteenth centuries, stood out against universal suffrage.

Despite its uniquely intolerable character, white South Africa appeared to believe for many years that it was entitled to special neglect from the West, to be allowed to go its own way simply because it had declared itself a part of the Western world. Illogically, it would demand special tolerance because of its anti-communism, while complaining that the West did not make a special case against Eastern bloc countries which also practised repression and coercion in the context of an absence of consent. This lament contained little truth. The West was in a state of cold war with the Soviet Union and its satellites for forty years from 1946. Far from the West not taking a strong line with Russian domestic repression and international destabilisation, almost all the efforts of the Western countries from the end of the Second World War were directed at this to the exclusion of much else. South African racism benefited from this almost monolithic concentration on the threat of communism. The fact of its now rising rather higher up the agenda of Western concern is in part a reflection of the decline in tension with the communist countries.

Simultaneous with this decline in tension with the East has been a resurgence in Western interest in more liberal economic arrangements. This has made South Africa of even greater interest. Just as, for instance, the whole of western Europe is moving to abolish its frontiers for labour market purposes, so that people may move freely, take jobs where they will, resettle their families, pursue their studies, enjoy their retirement, spend their leisure wherever and however they choose, South Africa is enforcing a directed labour market and has been creating new and bogus states, with frontiers, passports, visas and work permits. The fact that some clauses of the Group Areas Act, under which the homelands policy is administered, now go increasingly unenforced, adds to the administrative confusion and imposes further costs by depriving citizens of clear legal principles on which to base their social choices.

The prolonged social and intellectual isolation of white South Africans at the foot of Africa, where they have been free to practise their own brand of intolerance, has produced a situation in which, though they claim to belong to the Western community of nations, they seem to share little in common with it. As we shall see, they have created a strangely regulated economy, with in some sectors a misallocation of resources that amounts to profligacy, and in others a form of structural distortion that is making quite arduous both the taking and the implementing of rational economic decisions.

That they should be engaging in this at a time when so much of the rest of the world is seeking to rectify its economic management, and to pursue improved efficiency and more effective economic development, is little short of breath-taking.

The most obvious, and one of the most visible consequences of this divergence has been in South Africa's diplomatic, economic and military relations with its immediate neighbours in decolonised southern Africa. Instead of pursuing rational policies of economic growth through co-operation across national boundaries – which is the tendency elsewhere in the world – the policy of apartheid has led the South African government to favour policies designed to tie her immediate neighbours to a form of economic subservience, while employing a deceitful diplomacy coupled with military force to impose its political hegemony on the whole region.

South Africa's economic dominance in southern Africa is illustrated in Table 2.1. This dominance is not a central concern of this book, but it is important to grasp the sheer scale and magnitude of the economic weight that the Republic carries in comparison with its neighbours. It is of critical importance for future investment and growth in, for instance, Zimbabwe, that its economy should not be poisoned by the state of the South African economy.

Table 2.1 may require a little interpretation. For instance the figure in the final column giving South African per capita GDP of $2300, obscures the fact that if we take a 1983 exchange rate of R1.20 to US$1, then white GDP averaged $5202 per annum, while that of Africans resident in the homelands (who in 1980 constituted 53.7% of all blacks) averaged $323, which was actually no better than the average for the ten SADCC countries of southern Africa. It is important to remember also that behind these numbers there lies the reality of South African economic domination in practice: the same mining companies operating in the black African states; the transport network that ties those states to a relationship of dependence in international trade; the use of migrant labour to manipulate both their own

Table 2.1 Southern Africa: Area, Population and GDP Statistics, 1984

	Area (000 sq. km)	Population (millions)	Population density (persons/ sq. km)	GDP ($b)	As % of total	As % of SA's GDP	GDP per capita ($)
Angola	1247	9.9	8	4.7	4.85	6.40	470
Botswana	600	1.0	2	1.0	1.03	1.36	990
Lesotho	30	1.5	50	0.4*	0.41*	0.54*	240*
Malawi	118	6.8	58	1.1	1.14	1.55	160
Mozambique	802	13.4	17	2.8	2.89	3.81	210
Namibia	824	1.1	1	1.2	1.24	1.63	1100
Swaziland	17	0.7	41	0.6	0.62	0.82	770
Tanzania	945	21.5	23	4.4	4.55	6.00	200
Zambia	753	6.4	8	2.6	2.69	3.54	410
Zimbabwe	391	8.1	21	4.6	4.75	6.26	570
The ten	5727	70.4	12	23.4	24.17	31.88	330
South Africa	1221	31.6	26	73.4*	–	–	2300*
Southern Africa	6948	102.0	15	96.8	–	–	950

* These figures are for 1983.

Sources: Adapted from Lewis 1987; and Wilson & Ramphele 1989, 28.

domestic labour market and their diplomatic relations with neighbouring states, and so on.

The fact of South African intervention in its region, and the forms that that intervention has taken, have naturally focused the attention of the international community on it. The Commonwealth Secretariat has estimated, for instance, that Mozambique, in response to the terrorist attacks launched against it by South African financed rebels (the Mozambique National Resistance, MNR, or Renamo) as well as by the South African Defence Force (SADF) itself, was by 1985 having to devote 43% of its annual budget to defence and security. Destabilisation in Mozambique has included the destruction of transportation links and other aspects of the country's already limited infrastructure. What could be a rapidly developing country has had its progress blighted. In a study prepared in 1986 for the then President of Mozambique, Samora Machel, the Southern African Research and Documentation Centre estimated that between 1980 and 1985 the cost to Mozambique of South Africa's policy of destabilisation was somewhere between US$5.5 and US$6.5 billion. Since 1985 the situation has worsened, with war-related deaths in the country now believed to be in excess of 600,000 and the country threatened by famine. President Chissano of Mozambique has described the situation in his country as 'a monstrous crime which is reaching the proportions of genocide'. In September 1988, in a document prepared to coincide with the visit to Mozambique of the Pope, the Roman Catholic church of Mozambique explicitly accused South Africa of never having kept the Nkomati Accord of 1984, by which Mozambique pledged to cease support for the ANC and to expel it from its territory, in return for South Africa ceasing to finance the MNR. The Catholic church judged that 'South Africa has done very little to implement the letter and the spirit of the modus vivendi and has thus effectively transformed it into a modus moriendi'.

The white regime in South Africa, through its policies in the region, has become a menace to peace and security. Instead of being, from its position of economic strength and technical prowess, a motor for the dynamic growth of the poor countries of Africa south of the Sahara, it has become an impediment to their development. In its response to the challenge of underdevelopment in Africa, South Africa is bound to attract criticism from the West because Western governments favour effective strategies for development and are conscious of the burden of costs imposed on the international community by the continued failure to achieve them.

It has long been a principle of international diplomacy that one country does not interfere in the internal politics of another. The principle has, certainly throughout the period of the cold war, been much honoured in the breach. In the case of South Africa, disapproval turned first to criticism and then to condemnation. In the international financial community condemnation is now becoming rejection. However, the isolation that South Africa is experiencing as a result of this development has been brought about by the policy choices of its own government in the context of a rapidly changing domestic and international environment that it has never shown much capacity for understanding. The political, social and moral issues raised by these choices are too important for international opinion to ignore. As we have briefly surveyed them in this chapter, they include institutionalised racism; democratic legitimacy and the consent of the governed; constitutional gerrymandering; the rise of industrial and post-industrial conditions; the difficulty of achieving peaceful political transformation in a blocked setting; the knock-on effects of this difficulty to the international environment; the importance of history to the conduct of contemporary affairs; the evolution of East-West relations; economic liberalisation; military interventionism and regional destabilisation, and economic growth and development.

With a list of critical issues as long as this, surely it is small wonder that South Africa should now be seen by decision-makers and publics alike in the powerful communities of nations of the West as a special case, deserving of special treatment.

CHAPTER THREE

Recent Developments in the South African Economy

Economy and society are inseparable.

Apartheid, an aspect of society, is also a defining feature of the economy of South Africa, and one that South Africa can no longer afford. Apartheid has not contributed to a strengthening of South African society or economy, but has undermined the one and hobbled the other. It has meant that the talents of 80% of the population have been prevented from contributing fully to the collective welfare of the society and the strength of the economy.

In this chapter we examine the broad outlines of the current situation of the South African economy, illustrating its principal problems and explaining why they are unlikely to be solved under the current arrangements. The discussion is not formal, but it is slightly technical. To help in its digestion a few broad principles of political sociology are set out by way of introduction.

Social structure, broadly defined as the class, status and cultural elements of a society, and the ways in which they interact with each other, both flow from and contribute to the structure of the economy and how it is evolving. Thus it is impossible to think of social classes without making at least implicit assumptions about the economic structures in which they occur, and even when status systems may actually reflect aspects of society that have otherwise long since become defunct in practical terms, they are none the less being worked out in contemporary economic relationships.

South Africa under the social relations of apartheid is particularly vivid and explicit evidence of these facts. We are not in a position here to give even a summary of the historical evolution of apartheid, or to provide an account of the complex social relations to which it was a response and to which it has given rise. However, a number of broad points need to be put briefly and then kept in mind throughout the analysis that follows.

1 The segregation of the population of South Africa by race was not a response to demands imposed by the economy. In this sense there is nothing 'necessary' about racism whatsoever. On the contrary, many of the institutions of apartheid, such as the Group Areas Act and the former Pass Laws and job reservation system, work against the pursuit and achievement of efficient production and exchange in the economy as a whole, and so have inhibited rather than promoted normal economic development. This has been particularly the case in the labour market and the domestic capital market, two topics to which we return in greater detail below. (Lipton 1985, 227–54 contains a discussion of the controversy implicit in these remarks.)

2 It is implicit in our argument, from the principle that economy and society are inseparable, that any long-term attempt to develop and sustain a modern, developed economy on the basis of social institutions that are not congruent with the underlying requirements of modernity, cannot succeed. This is a complex field that would require another whole volume to fill out in detail. Put bluntly, however, industrial society presupposes industrial workers who will be both producers and consumers. A peasantry can perform a transitional role in the move from pre-industrial to industrial arrangements; thereafter it will have no place and will atrophy

if the industrial arrangements solidify and persist.

A post-industrial society, enormously more complex than its immediate predecessor, presupposes – indeed is partially defined by – the existence of a 'theory class': a mass public of highly educated people whose work and interests are largely abstract, producing and consuming the products of technology and the new service industries. It is not possible to sustain in the medium or long term a post-industrial economy in a society largely composed of a peasant class. Attempts to do so will necessarily be frustrated either by the absence of a sufficiently wealthy economic base, or a lack of suitable consumers for the products of such an economy, or insufficient investment resources, or bottlenecks in the supply of skilled and educated labour, or incongruous disjunctions between the cultural attachments of different segments of the population, or some combination of these phenomena.

Looked at in this way, the social relations of apartheid are not congruent with the economic requirements of either industrial or post-industrial production and exchange. This lack of congruity has exerted progressively more intense pressures on the society as a whole: pressures that find expression in politics, religion, relations at the workplace, decisions about investment and consumption, cultural events, and so on. These expressions are the daily fare of the media in South Africa (in so far as they are currently permitted to report them), but because of the complexity of the relationship between economy and society their causes may be subtle and obscure.

3 As Ralf Dahrendorf has so succinctly expressed it in the case of Germany (Dahrendorf 1968), there is the importance of history; what he calls the historicity of everything. Time's arrow is a merciless disciplinarian in the sense that it is impossible (as James II's grammarians knew) to undo those things that have been done, though we might still hope to be forgiven for them. In evolutionary terms, the 'selection' of any particular development strategy, through the process of recur-

sion, not only may lead to new possibilities but also cuts off whole avenues of alternative development. Put bluntly, once you have gone so far it is not possible to go back. It is the crisis generated by this underlying principle which now confronts South African economy and society.

4 It is almost a cliché of popular understanding that 'today's world' is 'one world'. It is not possible to be isolated from the world economy, or to be insulated from its products – from affluence to effluents. To pursue growth and improved standards of welfare is to belong to the world economy. To encounter difficulties in this pursuit is to require assistance from the international bodies that can facilitate them. South Africa, whatever some small minority of its citizens might wish, cannot opt out of the world: its own economy has evolved too far and the economic geography of the rest of the world now leaves the inhabitants of South Africa with no alternative but to wrestle with the problems that they have *in situ*. The white regime cannot go back to a nineteenth-century frontier economy, but neither can it go forward to a secure industrial future if that is to be based on apartheid. The evidence for this terrible dilemma lies in the current state of its economy.

Figures for changes in the real Gross Domestic Product (GDP) of the South African economy from 1982 to the present are set out in Table 3.1. They show that the recession of 1982 and 1983 was followed by a sharp increase in GDP in 1984. This expansion was followed by two more years of recession followed by one of modest expansion in 1987, with rapid growth occurring in the final quarter of that year and the first quarter of 1988. The seasonally adjusted annual rates of growth in those two quarters were 3.9% and 3.8% respectively.

This growth was the result of the government's economic policy response to the political and financial crisis of 1984–85, and was achieved through a combination of loose monetary policy and fiscal expansion leading to an increase in private consumption.

In principle the government of South Africa is committed

Table 3.1 Percentage Growth in Selected Components of Gross Domestic Product (constant 1985 prices)[a]

	1982	1983	1984	1985	1986	1987				1987	1988				1988
						I	II	III	IV		I	II	III	IV	
Private consumption	2.1	1.8	3.5	-3.6	0.8	1.3	4.7	4.2	4.8	3.6	4.9	4.8	5.5	3.9	4.8
General government consumption	5.5	1.6	7.7	3.4	2.2	27.6	3.6	-20.5	20.3	3.9	21.4	-13.7	-10.2	2.8	1.7
GDFI[b]	-2.9	-4.8	-2.0	-7.2	-17.9	9.3	-17.4	5.7	14.1	-2.8	8.8	4.0	7.1	8.6	6.4
Gross domestic expenditure	-5.6	-5.0	7.9	-7.8	0.1	25.0	6.3	9.3	4.2	4.1	23.0	1.2	-6.8	-0.2	7.0
Exports	0.1	-5.5	8.5	10.1	-1.4	2.1	-18.6	-12.7	21.2	-2.6	-5.0	12.0	26.3	19.4	5.7
Imports	-15.6	-17.1	20.3	-14.8	-2.6	128.8	-10.5	7.4	28.5	3.9	79.2	8.9	-10.6	11.0	22.5
GDP	-0.8	-2.1	5.1	-0.8	0.3	2.3	1.7	2.7	3.9	2.1	3.8	2.2	3.5	2.9	3.2

(a) Compared with the preceding year (or quarter); annual rates of change based on seasonally adjusted quarterly data.
(b) Gross Domestic Fixed Investment.

Source: SARB Quarterly Bulletin, December 1988, p. S112 for 1982; SARB Quarterly Bulletin, March 1989, p. S112 for 1983–1988.

to a medium-term objective of reducing the rate of inflation to 9% by 1991–92; to keeping its fiscal deficit below 3% of GDP, and to ensuring that budget revenues cover at least recurrent expenditure. In practice, however, it has attempted to maintain employment growth through fiscal expansion, and used monetary policy to influence the rate of growth in the short term, keeping interest rates low and only raising them when 'overheating' threatened serious balance of payments consequences. With the exception of 1978, real interest rates in South Africa were actually negative from 1973 to 1982 and again from mid-1985 to mid-1988 (see Figure 3.1).

One effect of using monetary policy as a short-term policy instrument is that it may involve frequent changes in interest rates, which may vary greatly in relatively short periods of time. In South Africa they varied by a whole 10 percentage points between the first quarter of 1984 and the first quarter of 1985, and by the same amount again between the same quarters of 1985 and 1986. This phenomenon produces sharp variations in the velocity of circulation of the money supply, which in turn makes the achievement of monetary targets very difficult. Thus in the year to May 1988 M3 grew at 22.7% when the Reserve Bank's target range was actually 12 to 16%.

The economic consequences of making medium-term policy objectives subservient to short-term considerations of this kind were compounded by the growth of public expenditure and the use of fiscal policy to promote growth. In 1986, 1987 and 1988 the government ran budget deficits of 4.2%, 5.7% and 5.0% (estimated) of GDP respectively, supplementing the growth of public sector activity with public sector wage increases that also helped to bolster domestic consumption.

Given this combination of policies, the GDP growth that was achieved in 1987–88 can only be characterised as weak when measured against South Africa's needs. Though it must have brought some benefits, it mainly served to highlight major areas of persistent economic vulnerability. The two most important of these are the fragility of the current account surplus (that is the difference between exports and imports of

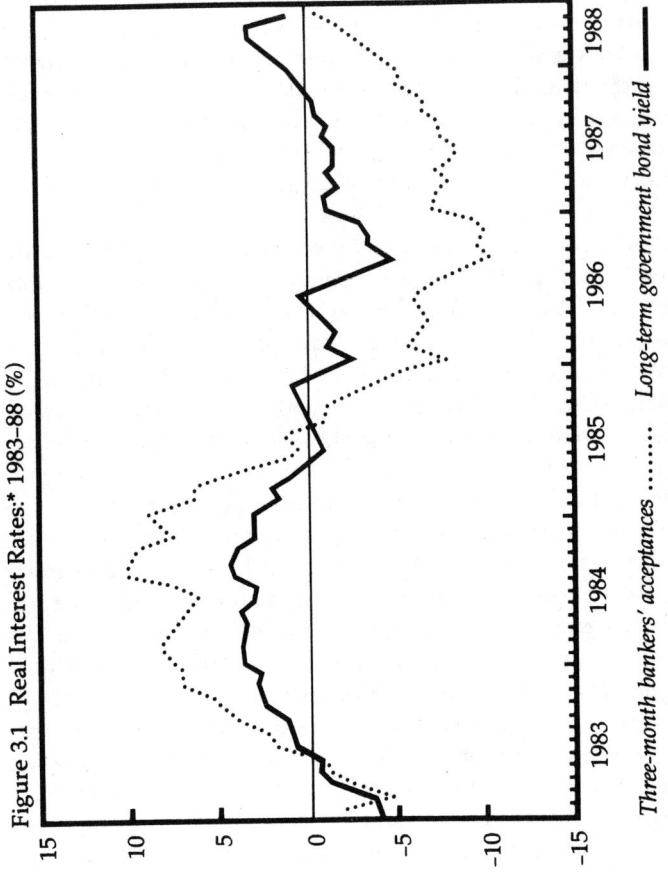

Figure 3.1 Real Interest Rates:* 1983–88 (%)

Three-month bankers' acceptances .... *Long-term government bond yield* ——

* Corrected for the change in consumer prices.

Source: SARB, Quarterly Bulletin.

goods and services) and the level of domestic savings and investment (that is the amount of local consumption forgone in order to replenish and expand the capital stock).

The weaknesses in these two areas of the economy are what cripples South Africa's capacity for sustained economic growth. In periods of expansion, when new wealth is being created and new employment opportunities are being added to the labour market, they compel the authorities to intervene by tightening policy and slowing the economy down. As a result they are of particular interest and need to be illustrated in a little detail. Tables 3.2 and 3.3 contain data on South Africa's balance of payments situation, 3.2 showing the annual balance of payments performance since 1980 and 3.3 the quarterly performance of the current account from 1986 to the first quarter of 1989.

What the data here suggest is that periods of rapid domestic growth lead to pressure on the balance of payments. In 1981 (with a lag into 1982), again in 1984 and again in the final quarter of 1987 and first quarter of 1988, strong domestic growth produced a sharp rise in imports, both by volume and value, which either put the current account firmly into deficit or threatened to do so until the authorities intervened to dampen domestic demand.

Since the political and economic crisis of 1985 the authorities have been conscious that the need to repay foreign debt would require them to maintain large surpluses on the current account. Export performance is vulnerable to the pattern of world growth (if it is weakening, and where), fluctuations in the gold price, and trade sanctions, while South African imports have usually grown more than proportionately during periods of economic recovery. Because of these factors it has been long understood that the external account functioned as a constraint on both the rate and the extent (depth and duration) of economic recovery.

Evidence of this constraint mounted throughout 1987 (Table 3.3). Non-gold merchandise exports peaked in the third quarter of 1986 and did not recover to that level again until the second

Table 3.2   Balance of Payments, 1980–88 (R millions)

	1980	1981	1982	1983	1984	1985	1986	1987	1988
A. MERCHANDISE TRADE									
Non-gold exports	9 766	9 579	10 142	10 207	12 907	20 465	25 048	25 145	31 472
Gold exports	10 141	8 340	8 627	9 929	11 684	15 460	16 719	17 792	19 622
Imports	-14 159	-18 111	-18 004	-15 863	-21 471	-23 045	-25 514	-28 320	-39 170
TRADE BALANCE	5 748	-192	765	4 273	3 120	12 880	16 253	14 618	11 924
% of GDP	(9.7)	(-0.2)	(1.0)	(5.0)	(3.1)	(11.3)	(12.3)	(9.3)	(6.2)
B. INVISIBLES									
Service receipts	2 761	3 084	3 506	3 565	4 441	5 796	6 222	6 453	7 504
Service payments	-5 984	-7 351	-7 955	-8 279	-10 119	-13 109	-15 664	-15 350	-16 822
Net transfers	293	370	339	363	338	358	385	431	393
Net invisibles	-2 930	-3 897	-4 110	-4 351	-5 340	-6 955	-9 057	-8 466	-8 925
CURRENT ACCOUNT BALANCE	2 818	-4 089	-3 345	-78	-2 220	5 925	7 196	6 152	2 939[a]
% of GDP	(4.5)	(-5.8)	(-4.2)	(-0.1)	(-2.1)	(4.9)	(5.2)	(3.7)	(1.5)
C. CAPITAL MOVEMENTS									
Net long-term capital	-478	542	2 433	-238	2 563	-445	-3 060	-1 698	-1 052
Net short-term capital	-1 804	419	797	290	-1 772	-8 786	-3 037	-1 371	-5 611
Net capital movements	-2 282	961	3 230	52	791	-9 231	-6 097	-3 069	-6 663
CHANGE IN NET FOREIGN RESERVES	536	-3 128	-125	-26	-1 429	-3 306	1 099	3 083	-3 724

[a] Apparent error in original source.

Source: SARB Quarterly Bulletins.

Table 3.3 Quarterly Current Accounts of Balance of Payments: Seasonally Adjusted Annual Rates, 1986–88 (R millions)

	1986				1987				1988			
	I	II	III	IV	I	II	III	IV	I	II	III	IV
A. MERCHANDISE TRADE												
Non-gold exports	20 211	24 270	28 635	27 076	23 882	24 468	24 810	27 224	26 300	29 282	33 830	36 476
Gold exports	15 780	16 069	18 038	16 989	18 390	17 043	17 911	17 824	18 530	19 948	20 230	19 780
Imports	-24 575	-24 364	-30 340	-22 777	-26 409	-27 370	-28 817	-30 684	-36 780	-38 310	-40 070	-41 520
TRADE BALANCE	11 416	15 975	16 333	21 288	15 863	14 141	13 904	14 564	8 050	10 920	13 990	14 736
% of GDP	8.8	11.9	11.4	14.1	10.2	8.8	8.4	8.3	4.3	5.6	6.9	7.0
B. INVISIBLES												
Service receipts	5 764	6 303	6 551	6 270	6 059	6 748	6 367	6 638	6 923	6 705	8 058	8 330
Service payments	-14 907	-16 442	-16 260	-15 047	-15 109	-15 498	-15 211	-15 582	-15 460	-16 394	-17 701	-17 973
Net transfers	346	493	333	368	419	445	420	440	429	517	273	353
Net invisibles	-8 797	-9 646	-9 376	-8 409	-8 631	-8 305	-8 424	-8 504	-8 108	-9 174	-9 370	-9 290
CURRENT ACCOUNT BALANCE	2 619	6 329	6 957	12 879	7 232	5 836	5 480	6 060	-58	1 748	4 620	5 446
% of GDP	2.0	4.7	4.9	8.5	4.7	3.6	3.3	3.5	-0.03	0.9	2.3	2.6

Source: SARB Quarterly Bulletin, March 1989, p. S66.

quarter of 1988; while imports continued to grow throughout 1987 and into 1988. The trade and current account balances peaked as a percentage of GDP in the fourth quarter of 1986 and then fell away. Despite this decline, the surplus on the current account in 1987 was R6.2 billion, and though smaller than 1986, was still bigger than most observers had expected. It enabled South Africa to meet its capital repayments and other capital outflows (see chapter four for a detailed discussion of the capital account), and also permitted some rebuilding of net foreign reserves, which by the end of the year amounted to the equivalent of three to four months of merchandise imports.

On the basis of this performance the expectation in early 1988 was for a further surplus on the current account, though perhaps of only half that of the previous year, with continuing GDP growth in the vicinity of 2.5% to 3.0%. In order to sustain this, the commercial banks expected that the authorities would have to allow some further depreciation of the Rand and impose a tighter fiscal policy to prevent the current account surplus getting any smaller than that.

In the event the current account pressures emerged much faster than had been expected. Table 3.4 gives the balance of payments quarterly figures (not adjusted) for 1987 and 1988. They show that the decline in the current account in the final quarter of 1987 accelerated in the new year. A sharp increase in domestic demand and stockbuilding produced a surge in real imports, while exports remained stagnant. In the March quarter, compared with the same period of the previous year, the trade balance fell by 40% to R2.77 billion, generating a current account surplus only one third what it had been a year earlier. At a seasonally adjusted annual rate this was equivalent to a balance of payments annual deficit of R58 million (Table 3.3).

Faced with this rapid deterioration in the current account the authorities moved to tighten monetary policies, with the SARB raising its minimum lending rate from 9.5% to 10.5% in March, to 11.5% in May, to 12.5% in July, and to 14.5% in

Table 3.4 Current Account, 1987–88: Quarterly Figures (R millions – current prices: seasonally unadjusted)

| | 1987 | | | | 1988 | | | |
	I	II	III	IV	I	II	III	IV
Merchandise trade								
Exports	10 949	9 879	11 169	10 941	11 346	11 669	14 193	13 886
Imports	6 353	6 686	7 412	7 869	8 578	9 468	10 444	10 680
Trade balance	4 596	3 193	3 757	3 072	2 768	2 201	3 749	3 206
Net invisibles	-2 088	-2 108	-2 160	-2 190	-1 844	-2 488	-2 341	-2 312
Current account balance	2 588	1 085	1 597	882	924	-287	1 408	894

Source: SARB Quarterly Bulletin, March 1989, p. S65.

November. In his budget of 1 April 1988 the Finance Minister, Barend du Plessis, forecast a reduction equivalent to 1% of GDP in the government's fiscal deficit.

The lesson was reasonably clear: the government had employed expansionary demand management policies to stimulate economic activity in the wake of the economic and political events of 1984 and 1985. However, these policies proved insufficient, on their own, to create sustainable GDP growth in excess of about 2.0% without exerting pressure on the current account of the balance of payments. Normally any reasonably healthy economy would make up the difference through its capital account, importing capital to cover the deficit on the current account and employing the time purchased in this way to pursue the structural adjustment that may lead to external surpluses in the future.

South Africa, however, could not follow this path because it had been forced to become a net exporter of capital. As a direct result of the political and social unrest produced by the policies of apartheid, foreign investors withdrew their funds, domestic companies and individuals postponed investment plans and exported their capital, and international financial markets successively closed their doors to South African borrowers. (These matters are dealt with in detail in chapters four, five and six.) The effect of this combination of circumstances is that South Africa's need to meet its debt servicing and repayment obligations in the absence of any significant capital in-flows, means that it cannot afford to run a current account deficit, and so must be content with low rates of growth.

This has been very hard for the authorities to accept because they badly need growth to create employment for their rapidly expanding population. Figures on population growth in southern Africa vary somewhat from source to source, and in common with those from less-developed countries have to be treated with caution. The overall picture is reasonably clear, however, and is set out in Tables 3.5 and 3.6.

The population of South Africa rose by five million in the ten years from 1965 to 1974 (this is the cohort that has come

Table 3.5   Population Growth, 1965–85

	Total (m)	% increase	Average annual increase over previous period
1965	19.61		
1970	22.47	14.6	2.76
1975	25.47	13.35	2.56
1980	28.61	12.33	2.34
1985	32.39	13.21	2.5

Source: UN population statistics.

Table 3.6   Population Growth by Racial Community, 1960–85[a]

	Black	Coloured	White
1960	2.3	2.8	1.7
1970	3.4	3.1	2.1
1980	2.7	2.1	1.5
1985	3.4	2.1	1.6

[a] Percentage changes are average annual increases since the previous census.

Source: South Africa Year Book, 1985; Pretoria: Bureau of National and International Communications; Africa: South of the Sahara 1988. London: Europa.

onto the labour market since 1980), by a further five million in the seven years to 1981 and by a further five million again in the six years after that. The annual growth rate in population has been at or close to 2.5% for the last thirty years, but far higher among the black population than the white. In 1980 almost 60% of the total population of South Africa was under the age of twenty-five. In 1989 reasonably reliable estimates suggest that half of the black population is under the age of fifteen. The current population will, by the year 2000 (that is, this is not a forecast based on the linear extrapolation of fertility rates, but a projection from the current population of persons aged between four and fifty) provide South Africa with a labour force estimated at eighteen million. The employed workforce today is approximately seven million.

Some figures which project population size into the twenty-first century on the basis of current fertility rates are set out in Table 3.7.

Table 3.7   Projected Population at Current Growth Rates, 1980–2004

	% growth per annum	1980	2000	2020	2040
			Year		
Black	2.80	20.70	36.40	65.60	121.19
White	1.55	4.40	5.81	6.64	7.03
Coloured	1.80	2.53	3.79	5.40	7.57
Indian	1.76	0.81	1.16	1.55	1.99
TOTAL	2.66	28.44	47.16	79.19	137.78

Source: Leach 1986, 242.

These figures must be treated with caution. Firstly, as with the statistics in Table 3.6, the figures for 1980 are Republic of South Africa figures, which exclude the populations of the independent homelands. They therefore understate the size of the black population. (Compare with the UN figures in Table 3.5.)

Secondly, the linear projection of population growth is a notoriously unreliable method of forecasting. There is evidence that the annual percentage increase in the South African black population is now falling. We include the table out of interest, however, because statistics of this kind have been widely publicised in South Africa in recent years, and are having a dynamic effect on the shaping of public opinion.

Whatever the true size of the population, the size of the labour force at the turn of the century (barring some catastrophic development such as a deadly epidemic) is, as we have said, already known because it has already been born. Estimates vary on how much annual growth of GDP will be required to generate sufficient employment for such a rapidly growing labour force. One source (Blumenfeld 1987a, 24–5) suggests that 'sustained output growth of at least 6% per annum will be needed if the current explosive rise in black unemployment is to be halted, let alone reversed'. Another (Dostall, quoted in Wilson & Ramphele 1989, 247) argues that a 'reasonably favourable' growth rate of 4.5% over the twenty years from 1980 to 2000 would create a labour market of just over twelve million jobs. Our own earlier estimate (Inter-governmental Group 1988, 7) that annual increases in GDP of 3.5% to 4.0% would be necessary to prevent further increases in unemployment, is certainly the low end of the range. It is also thought to be close to the minimum target the South African government has set for itself. One South African banking source suggested to us that growth rates in the 7.5% to 8.5% range would be necessary 'over ten to twelve years' to get unemployment down to acceptable (Western) levels.

The debate about growth and the likely level of job numbers that it may deliver is slightly artificial, however, since there are different kinds of growth. Clearly what the South African economy needs is growth in labour-intensive industries, where annual increases in GDP would be accompanied by greater employment opportunities. Unfortunately this does not appear to be the kind of growth that South Africa is now experiencing.

This was not always the case. From 1945 to 1975, with the exception of a brief dip in the mid-1950s, the rate of increase of employment outside the agricultural sector increased at least as fast as the black population. Since then, however, it has failed to keep pace with black population growth and in some years has actually fallen absolutely. Since 1980 employment in the non-agricultural sector has grown by only about 5%, while the total workforce has grown by almost 20%. In the agricultural sector, and over a longer period of time, employment has declined absolutely, the number of black agricultural workers dropping from 750,000 in 1962 to 550,000 in 1980 – a decline of 26.6%.

In this context of shrinking job opportunities, one reasonable estimate for unemployment, measured in full-time job equivalents, was that it rose from 11.8% in 1970 to 15% in 1976, and 21.1% in 1981 (Simkins 1982, quoted in Wilson & Ramphele 1989, 235). No comparable statistics exist for the years since, as official data for registered unemployed exclude blacks outside the urban areas. The partial figures that are available show that unemployment among whites, coloureds and Indians rose from 0.7% in 1981 to 3.1% in 1987. Over the same period unemployment among urban blacks rose from 7.7% to 15.9%.

Much of the literature deals with this problem by simply ascribing it to the fact that the South African economy has two sectors: a formal sector and an informal sector. In the formal sector there is employment, taxation, welfare (though not much), and all the measured characteristics of a developed economy. In the informal sector (which no one has yet dared to call the black economy) there is surely economic activity, even if only of the barest subsistence kind, but none of it is measured. One unofficial estimate that we have seen suggests that the real GDP of South Africa may be as much as a third higher than is generally supposed, because the reported figure measures only the economic activity of the formal sector.

That large numbers of potential workers are unemployed remains beyond dispute. What is fairly keenly debated is the reasons for it. Broadly speaking, the explanations fall into two schools: those who argue that investment in capital-intensive industries has diminished job opportunities (this is the sub-stitution theory: that capital has been substituted for labour because of being relatively cheaper); and those who argue the scale effect, that cheaper capital leads to increased output and greater employment, that low interest rates in South Africa have coincided with rapidly rising employment opportunities, and that the explanation for rising unemployment must therefore lie elsewhere. Put bluntly, this theory proposes that falls in the rate of growth of the demand for labour occur as a result of falls in the rate of economic growth in general, and not as a result of an increase in the capital intensity of production.

There appears to be evidence for both points of view in the South African economy. Mechanisation and technical change in the agricultural sector have greatly reduced the labour intensity of farming (Wilson & Ramphele 1989, 240 *et seq*). Similar developments have no doubt reduced employment opportunities in other sectors. The country has also been experiencing historically low rates of growth. South Africa's growth of real GDP has fallen from an annual average of 5.8%

in the 1960s to 3.3% in the 1970s, to 1.8% in the eight years to 1987. In 1987 real GDP per head grew only 0.3% after declining in four of the preceding five years, and real personal disposable income per head fell by an average of 2.1% in each of the three years from 1985 to 1988.

At the same time as the amount of growth has been diminishing, its nature has been changing. In the twenty-eight years from 1960 the proportion of GDP growth arising from exports and domestic fixed investment has steadily declined, while that arising from private consumption has risen. In the 1960s private consumption accounted for 42% of the growth of GDP (and almost 50% of GDP itself): by 1988 it accounted for 80% of the GDP growth (and almost 55% of GDP).

Despite the persuasive evidence to support the scale-effect theory, it has also to be admitted that South African capital markets have evolved in response to the social policy of apartheid, and that some aspects of this evolution surely inhibit the creation of employment. Some examples follow. Restrictions on the educational opportunities available to non-whites mean that there is a scarcity of skilled labour. This scarcity is made worse by the *de facto* prohibition of black workers from certain 'whites only' jobs, even where formal job reservation for whites has been abolished. As a result of the bottlenecks, and the high wages for skilled jobs that have been created by these policies, investment has been directed away from labour-intensive towards capital-intensive activities (the substitution effect).

On the other hand, negative real interest rates have discouraged saving, and what saving there has been has been misdirected by government regulation. This has constrained the level and efficiency of investment and thus reduced the rate of economic growth. The tax system in South Africa encourages saving through insurance companies, pension funds and mortgage institutions. Insurance and pension funds have been required by law to invest very heavily in public-sector debt. The proportion of total saving left for risk-taking private business investment is relatively low. Other regulations make it virtually impossible for black people to gain access to commercial loans to start or to develop their own businesses (that is access to capital markets is not free), and there are regulations having to do with the evaluation of what constitutes capital gain which discourage capital transactions.

These forms of segmentation in the capital market have produced distortions that make very difficult precisely the kind of labour-intensive growth that is urgently required. They only exist because of apartheid.

Despite the stimulant of low interest rates, investment has been falling. Real gross domestic investment fell six years in a row from 1982 to 1987; net domestic investment by private businesses was actually negative in 1985 and 1986, and the ratio of real gross domestic fixed investment to GDP fell from 27.1% in 1982 to 18.7% in 1987. Although real gross domestic fixed investment rose by 6.7% in 1988, this was – as the SARB *Bulletin* pointed out – from a low base after six years of decline. It was still 27% lower than in the peak year of 1981, and there were signs that it was falling off rapidly towards the end of the year.

This weakness in investment is evidence of the extent to which private business confidence has ebbed away. For a quarter of a century, from 1946 to 1971, investment growth was greater than consumption growth. Now the refusal to invest (it has been referred to as 'internal disinvestment') is becoming a progressively more binding constraint as the stock of capital wears out and becomes obsolete, and as the numbers of the unemployed grow ever larger.

These difficulties are all then subjected to what we might, with a little irony, call the multiplier effect of the labour market consequences of the policy of apartheid. There has been so much talk in Western societies in recent years about the benefits of labour-market deregulation, the need for markets to be transparent so that the signals can be read correctly and the markets clear rapidly, that it is possible that we have lost our intuitive understanding for what it is like to be engaged in an economy in which the labour market is not free even in the most minimal sense. If you are black in South Africa you may not own land. You are meant not to live in a designated white area. The vast majority of workers in the mining industry (which employs approximately a twelfth of all workers in the formal sector) are recruited on a contract basis, and must live in all-male hostels, poorly accommodated, without their families. Skilled manual positions, white collar jobs, the opportunity to train for promotion, in short all the normal elements of Western industrial society, are still sometimes closed to black people, even if they can attain the educational prerequisites in the first place. Factory workers generally have to live far away from their places of work, and travel great distances every day. The Group Areas Act of 1950, still in force, which built on the residential segregation provisions of urban legislation of 1923, has disrupted and grossly distorted the labour market, and introduced the most extraordinary distortions into the economic life of the entire country, from the pattern of public expenditure at the national level to the physical fitness of individual workers to perform their daily labour effectively at the individual level.

To take an example that deserves to become notorious, since it sums up a very great deal of what is economically unusual about apartheid, we can look at the new 'homeland' of KwaNdebele (Wilson & Ramphele 1989, 212–15).

KwaNdebele is situated between 110 and 150 kilometres north-east of Pretoria, and was created in the 1970s to accommodate the rapidly increasing numbers of black people who, being forced off commercial (white-owned) farms, and with nowhere else to go, would otherwise have moved into the cities. The population of the area was 20,000 in 1970; by the mid-1980s it was anywhere from 300,000 to 500,000. Since there are very few jobs in KwaNdebele, the only hope of employment is either to get a work contract, say in a mine, in which case you must leave your family behind and be away for months on end, or become a 'pendelaar' (literally, a 'shuttle'), and travel every day by bus to Pretoria for work. Some, who may have as much as four hours of travel each way, will leave home at 3 a.m. and get home again at 9 p.m. The great growth industry in the region of KwaNdebele and Pretoria is the bus service.

In the 1988–89 budget, a sum of R400 million was appropriated to subsidise bus 'commuter' services. In the same year, for the upgrading of residential housing in black areas, the sum appropriated was R106 million.

The investment and job-creation opportunities that are being forgone as a result of this kind of structural distortion beggar the imagination. The benefits in production, employment, growth, consumption and welfare that would flow simply from allowing the planned development of residential neighbourhoods close to expanding centres of employment are obvious enough. Instead, apartheid subsidises buses.

This is what economists mean when they talk about distortion and the misallocation of resources. (See also Savage 1986, who has attempted to add up the cost of apartheid under seven separate headings: direct costs, indirect costs, enforcement costs, lost-opportunity costs, punitive costs, human costs, and regional costs. His exercise lies outside the scope of this book, but is surely worth pursuing in more detail.)

A regime that is prepared to waste resources in this way is clearly not one that is going to shy away from public expenditure growth or the increases in taxation that go with it. Public expenditure now accounts for almost 28% of GDP, and public sector employment, broadly defined, accounts for approximately a third of the workforce in the formal sector. In 1987, when constraints on public sector growth were supposedly being rigorously enforced, public sector employment actually grew by 9%. The overall levels of public expenditure and employment are not high by OECD standards, but they are high by developing country standards, and they also are suggestive of a trend which surely cannot be sustained.

A very large proportion of the continuous public sector expenditure growth is generated by apartheid: the numerous layers of politics and bureaucracy (each racial group being separately serviced); the duplicate, sometimes triplicate programs; the military and police costs associated with social control and repression; the rise in 'justice' and prison costs under the state of emergency; the costs of law enforcement under the Group Areas Act, and much else besides. As a single but telling example, Savage (1986, 9) has calculated that there are 151 separate government departments in South Africa, and that '[t]he fragmentation of services has produced a patchwork of badly co-ordinated and overlapping services'. Cautiously, he comments that 'The economic costs of running 151 Departments, each having separate managerial and administrative staff, separate budgets, separate accounting procedures and often providing duplicated facilities and services is difficult to probe'.

The burden of all this expenditure falls on the tax system, plus the public sector borrowing requirement to make up any shortfall. Taxes have risen continuously throughout the decade. The General Sales Tax (GST) was raised in steps from 4% in 1980 to 12% in 1988, and is now to be replaced with a new, higher Value Added Tax (VAT). Tax concessions for non-mining companies have been continuously tightened. Fiscal drag, in the context of high inflation, has been allowed to take a growing proportion of personal incomes. The effect of the rising personal tax burden and of high inflation at a time when GDP growth has become more dependent on personal consumption has meant that consumers could only maintain that consumption at the cost of reducing their savings. Figures for this are set out in Table 3.8.

The ratio of personal saving to personal disposable income was only 2.8% in 1987, and actually fell through the course of the year from 3.9% in the first quarter to 2.3% in the fourth. In the March quarter of 1988 it went down again, to 1.8%. As we have seen, however, this weakening of personal savings has been dwarfed by the deterioration in the savings performance of general government (that is the central government, plus provincial administrations and local authorities), which has been a net dis-saver since 1982, running large budget deficits to counteract the economic consequences of the political

Table 3.8   Personal Consumption and Saving, 1960–88

	1960–69	1970–79	1980–88
A. ANNUAL GROWTH RATES (%)			
Current income	8.8	14.2	16.8
Direct taxation	12.1	16.2	23.6
Personal disposable income	8.6	14.0	15.8
Inflation	2.4	9.9	14.7
Real personal disposable income	6.0	4.2	1.3
Real personal disposable income per capita	3.3	1.6	-1.3
Real private consumption expenditure	5.1	3.6	3.0
B. PERSONAL SAVINGS RATIO (%)[a]	11.3	10.2	4.6

[a] Personal saving as a percentage of personal disposable income.

Source: Sanlam Economic Survey, April 1988, p. 6, updated to include 1988
figures using SARB Quarterly Bulletin, March 1989, passim.

unrest arising from its policies of apartheid. The figures are set out in Table 3.9.

Strong growth in net corporate savings was insufficient to offset these weaknesses, so that gross domestic savings, which had stood at 25.5% of GDP in 1985 fell to 23.3% in 1987 and to 21.6% in the first quarter of 1988. These figures are in contrast with gross domestic savings ratios of almost 30% throughout the 1960s and 1970s.

Nor is this situation likely to be reversed in the short term, given the high rates of inflation that have been experienced in South Africa over the past ten years. The figures, including comparisons with South Africa's main trading partners, are set out in Table 3.10 and Figure 3.2.

What they show is that South Africa's rate of inflation, year on year, has not been below 10% throughout the entire decade, and that from the middle of 1985 to the beginning of 1988 the inflation rate exceeded that of South Africa's main trading partners by in excess of 10%. The figure for 1988 is lower largely because of a slowdown in the growth of import prices (which fell from 23.5% in 1985 to 9.7% in 1987) brought about by an increase in the effective exchange rate of the Rand. That is, as

Table 3.9 Financing of Gross Domestic Investment, 1980–88 (R millions – current prices)

	1980	1981	1982	1983	1984	1985	1986	1987	1988
Personal saving[a]	4 306	1 167	1 032	1 298	2 650	4 588	2 529	4 645	1 907
Corporate saving[a]	7 132	7 072	3 850	7 969	7 062	7 594	9 004	9 667	9 737
Saving of general government[a]	2 026	1 845	191	169	–1 111	–871	–1 274	–3 658	–1 064
Provision for depreciation[b]	8 194	9 860	12 215	14 461	16 386	19 947	25 059	28 499	32 785
GROSS DOMESTIC SAVING[c]	21 658	19 944	17 288	23 897	24 987	31 258	35 318	39 153	43 365
Net capital inflow from the rest of the world	–2 284	3 084	3 256	1 159	1 333	–7 160	–8 380	–4 236	–4 738
Use of gold and other foreign reserves	–534	1 005	89	–1 081	887	1 235	1 184	–1 916	1 799
GROSS DOMESTIC INVESTMENT	18 840	24 033	20 633	23 975	27 207	25 333	28 122	33 001	40 426

[a] After provision for depreciation and after inventory valuation adjustment.
[b] At replacement value.
[c] After inventory valuation adjustment.

Source: SARB *Quarterly Bulletins*, March 1988 and March 1989, p. S100.

Table 3.10   Percentage Increases in Consumer Prices, 1978–88
              (year on year)

	South Africa	Japan	United Kingdom	France	Germany	USA
1978	10.2	4.2	8.3	9.2	2.7	7.6
1979	13.1	3.7	13.4	10.7	4.1	11.3
1980	13.8	7.7	18.0	13.3	5.4	13.5
1981	15.3	4.9	11.9	13.3	6.3	10.4
1982	14.7	2.8	8.6	12.0	5.2	6.1
1983	12.3	1.9	4.6	9.4	3.3	3.2
1984	11.7	2.2	5.0	7.7	2.4	4.3
1985	16.2	2.0	6.1	5.8	2.2	3.5
1986	18.5	0.6	3.5	2.5	-0.3	1.9
1987	16.1	0.0	4.2	3.3	0.3	3.6
1988	13.2	0.7	4.9	2.7	1.1	4.1

Source: IMF international financial statistics, May 1989.

the Rand appreciated against other currencies, so the price of imports declined. The effect of this, of course, was the upsurge in imports that we have already discussed, leading to intense pressure on the balance of payments, and a consequent sequence of measures designed to dampen demand. Reflecting international concern at the sharp increase in imports, the Rand began to depreciate once more, reversing the trend in import prices. Inflation for the year to December 1988 was 13.2%, but rising, and expected to be back in the 15% to 18% range for 1989.

Solutions to these economic problems are clearly not easy to find. One possibility that the regime has clung to in hope over the past few years is that there will be an increase in the world price of gold. Gold is so important to the South African economy, and contributes so much to its balance of payments, taxation, and investment requirements, that a recovery in the price to say US$486.60 – which was the average price in December 1987 – if it persisted for several years, might provide a sufficient breathing space for economic recovery. (In early June 1989 the price was US$120 below that.) According to this view, big new surpluses on the current account would permit the repayment of outstanding debt. This in turn would

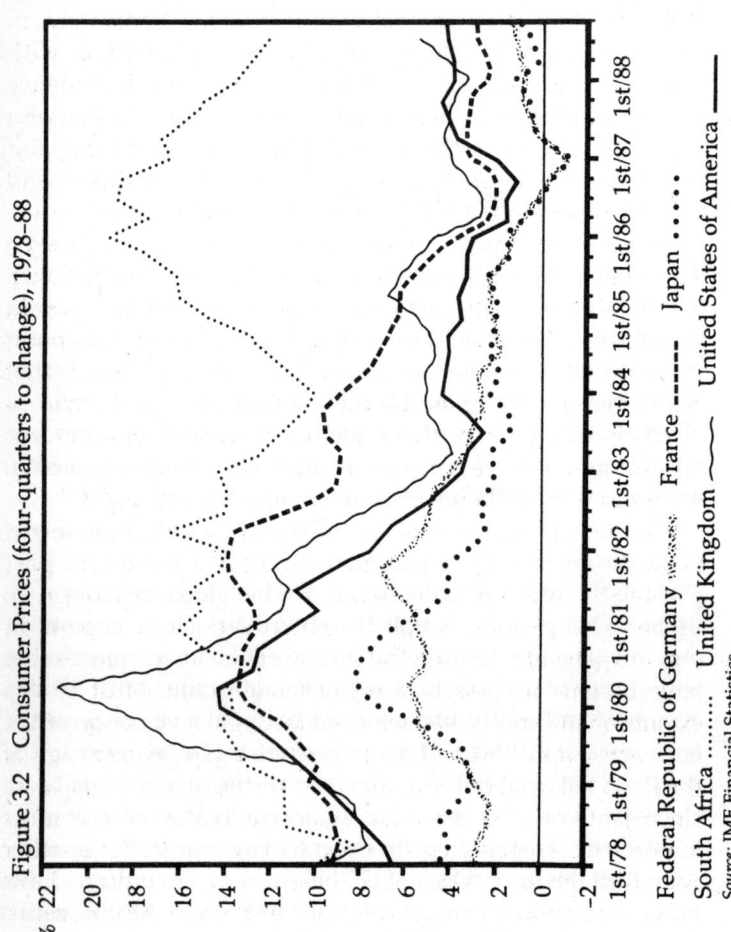

Figure 3.2 Consumer Prices (four-quarters to change), 1978–88

Federal Republic of Germany .... France ------ Japan •••••

South Africa .... United Kingdom —— United States of America ——

Source: IMF Financial Statistics.

rehabilitate South Africa in international capital markets and also provide the scope for more expansionary domestic policies without fears of external account deficits. Renewed high rates of growth would stimulate employment and investment, leading to a more stable socio-political environment.

The role that might be played by gold, given this scenario, is so important in the overall context of the political economy of South Africa that we deal with it in detail, separately, in chapter seven. Suffice it to say here that (in common with analysts in the industry) we have not found much evidence to support the possibility of either a rapid, a substantial or a sustained increase in the price of gold in the short term, and that furthermore, analysis suggests that the medium- and long-term prospects for the South African gold-mining industry are rather uncertain. Nor would it necessarily be the case, even if the gold price did apparently come to the rescue of the South African economy, that the repayment of external debt would be sufficient to reverse the outflow of capital. The whole point about this phenomenon, as we explain in chapter four, is that it is being brought about by the political and social environment generated by apartheid, and not by international perceptions of inherent weaknesses in the South African economy. We return to this theme in more detail in chapter eight.

A second possible solution to the economic difficulties might lie in the expansion of non-gold exports. In the recent past (1984-86) South Africa achieved a prodigious expansion in its non-gold exports coupled with reductions in imports in order to generate the large balance of payments surpluses that have become necessary to repay foreign debt. Most of this expansion in exports was achieved through devaluation of the currency. From 1984 to 1986 the effective rate of exchange of the Rand fell by about 35%, and over the eight and a half years since January 1981 its value against a basket of the most important currencies has dropped by two-thirds. Put another way, throughout 1980 one US dollar would, on average, have purchased approximately seventy-eight South African cents. In December 1988 US$1 was worth almost exactly R2.50. (A discussion of exchange rate fluctuations is included in chapter five, and exchange rate figures for 1981 to 1988 are set out in Table 5.2.)

The effect of further radical depreciation on non-gold export volumes is difficult to evaluate. In some sectors, such as diamonds and strategic minerals, South Africa's importance in the world market is so great that it would be difficult for it substantially to increase the volume of exports without depressing the price, which would defeat the object of the exercise. In some sectors of non-strategic and non-gemstone minerals however, where South Africa may be an important but not a principal supplier to world markets, it could – provided capacity constraints could be overcome – increase the volume of its external trade without influencing prices downwards. There has been evidence about South African coal exports to Spain to suggest that this might have been happening recently. According to reports in Spanish newspapers at the end of May 1989 the International Confederation of Free Trade Unions (ICFTU) believed that Spanish purchases of South African coal had risen from 371,000 tonnes in 1981 (5.3% of coal imports) to 4.45 million tonnes in 1988 (50.9% of imports). This expansion has been in contrast to the coal import figures for the members of the European Community as a whole, the proportion of whose imports of coal coming from South Africa has fallen from 26.8% in 1981 to 16% in 1988, though there have been persistent suspicions of blended and mislabelled South African coal arriving in Western Europe through Rotterdam. Spanish purchasers are believed also to be on-selling South African coal to other consumers. However, data on South African exports are incomplete, and it is not possible to say whether these figures represent an increase in production and supply or merely a substitution of one market (in and through Spain) for another (the other countries of the European Community). Generally speaking, capacity constraints have the effect of making very rapid sustainable increases in mineral production very difficult to achieve.

Other sectors of the South African economy present even

fewer opportunities for export expansion. Manufactured and agricultural products are not only subject to capacity constraints, like minerals, but also to the fact that, even without sanctions, it can take many years to build successful export markets. In any event, expansion in levels of capacity requires new investment, but the overall atmosphere for investment remains poor. As we have seen, gross domestic fixed investment remains weak (despite an increase in 1988), and it is still only at about the level reached in the mid-1970s. Moreover, it is hard to see how substantial new investment could be financed out of depressed domestic savings without new foreign capital inflows. The fact appears to be that any expansion of manufacturing and agricultural capacity to produce greater volumes for export depends on the reversal of recent trends in savings and investment. There is little evidence that this reversal is about to occur, and even if it did its effects would take several years to be felt.

In the absence of short-term solutions derived from increased export revenue, South African economists and politicians have turned to the possibility of medium- and long-term policies of structural adjustment. There has been a Commission of Inquiry into the Tax Structure (the Margo Commission) which brought down wide-ranging proposals for a more efficient and effective taxation system. A Committee of Inquiry into Taxation in the Mining Industry (the Marais Committee) has produced proposals for encouraging investment and expanded production in gold mining (see chapter seven). Attention has turned to the possibility of 'inward development', allowing a faster expansion of the informal sector of the economy by deregulation. The hope is that because the informal sector makes no use of imports, its growth will have no impact on the balance of payments. This remains a hope, however, for although there is anecdotal evidence of, for instance, the authorities turning a blind eye in some communities to such otherwise currently illegal activities as hawking, or unlicensed transport services (taxis and mini-buses) the reality is that any serious attempt to foster legal and legitimate growth in the informal sector necessarily entails the dismantling of apartheid.

In his speech opening parliament on 5 February 1988 the State President, P. W. Botha, indicated that his attention was focused elsewhere by introducing a program of structural reform that included deregulation in the formal sector and the privatisation of public enterprises and corporations.

This last proposal, though it is almost irrelevant to the economic situation of the black population, is particularly radical. The public sector, broadly defined, employs approximately 1.7 million workers, and the public corporations are a substantial and politically important element of the South African economy. They account for over 20% of value added and approximately 16% of the non-agricultural labour force. There are more than seventy public corporations engaged in everything from transport to iron and steel production, and they have always been a bastion of middle-class, white-collar Afrikaner employment, and voter support for the National Party. The sector has enjoyed virtual monopoly control of many industries, and has functioned as a sort of sheltered workshop or affirmative action program for Afrikaners through the application of its monopoly rents to finance extensive and well-paid employment.

Converting these enterprises and corporations into profit-seeking, tax-paying operations, and then privatising some of them would, if vigorously pursued, amount to a serious attack on many of the government's own supporters in the cause of greater efficiency and dynamism in the broader economy. Given that elections are to be held in early September 1989, perhaps it is hardly surprising that little of practical significance has been heard about these proposals in the eighteen months since they were announced.

According to the original conception, the proceeds from privatisation were to be employed to retire public debt and to develop infrastructure and small businesses. However, in the absence of capital inflows it is not easy to see where the capital is to come from to finance private-sector purchases.

Some observers believe that the impetus behind privatisation reforms is increasing fear of sanctions, which have tended to be directed in the first instance at government- and state-owned bodies (Hirsch forthcoming, 23). There may be some long-term strategic economic purpose in the privatisation proposals, but unless the term is very long indeed it is hard not to see in them at least some element of pre-emptive reform directed at expanding the private sector in advance of any possibility of power sharing with the currently disenfranchised majority of blacks. Both the ANC and the UDF, in principle, are committed to policies of widespread public ownership.

In the shorter term, Botha also announced in his speech that there would be a freeze on all public-sector salaries throughout 1988 which, given that inflation was then running at 14% and was rising, also amounted to a direct attack on the real incomes of Afrikaners.

Perhaps this was the explanation for the fact that in late September 1988, a month before the municipal elections, the State President announced significant public-sector wage increases to take effect from 1 January 1989. Public servants received 15% increases, and there were similar increases in social, civil and military pensions. Teachers were awarded 22%. The increases were somewhat higher than the 1988 inflation rate (13.2%) and added an extra R3.5 billion to the budget. When asked how the government would fund the increases, the Finance Minister, du Plessis – who was away from South Africa at the time of the announcement – said that he had no idea. In the context of wage increases for white state employees, and the lack of budgetary discipline entailed, it is perhaps worth remembering that the heaviest burden from the effects of inflation over the past decade has fallen on the vast majority of the population who are poor and politically powerless, and for whom the experience has been little short of 'devastating' (Wilson & Ramphele 1989, 249–53).

Important as the various proposals for economic reform may eventually turn out to be, they necessarily lie in the future, while the current state of the South African economy is a matter of grave concern now. In essence, the problems are easy enough to grasp. At a time when, because of capital outflows, South Africa has been thrown back on its own savings for investment, its savings performance has deteriorated. The economic distortions inherent in apartheid, the political and social unrest that has been reaching the proportions of turmoil, the existence of sanctions which along with the social disturbances have weakened business and investor confidence: these things combined have seriously reduced the capacity of the economy to perform efficiently. Poor economic policies, in which medium-term objectives have been consistently sacrificed for short-term expedience, have led to negative real interest rates and high and persistent inflation in a context of continuous devaluation. The result is a balance of payments impasse in which growth cannot be achieved at precisely the historical moment when growth and high levels of employment creation are essential to the future livelihood of the vast majority of the population.

When economic problems become so grave that they threaten the very fabric of society, the solutions to them are not purely technical economic ones. Economy and society are inseparable. Economic reform, under the duress of possible disaster, first requires the political will. There have been signs for some time that leading economic decision-makers inside South Africa now understand this fact. Speaking to the Institute of Life and Pension Advisers in Cape Town on 8 May 1989, Reserve Bank Governor Gerhard de Kock said:

South Africa's economic future is inextricably entwined with its political future. Continued political and constitutional reform and the maintenance of law and order are preconditions for the attainment of such economic ideals as optimal real growth, low single-digit inflation, balance of payments equilibrium, a strong currency and, in general, economic prosperity and a rise in the standard of living. Given the intensified stresses and strains in South Africa's political relationship with the rest of the world during the past four years . . . one would have thought that this proposition was self-evident. But this does not seem to be the case.

We will return to this theme in the final part of the book. First, however, we must examine the financial aspects of those 'intensified stresses and strains' to see how and why they have mattered so much.

Part II

CHAPTER FOUR

The Financial Crisis of 1985 and Beyond

South Africa has not been a heavy borrower of foreign capital in recent years. International bankers tend to see South Africa as a developing economy, and therefore, like other developing economies, in need of substantial capital transfers for investment purposes. Under the apartheid of recent years, however, what development there has been has largely been financed by domestic savings. Capital inflows, accounting for only about 0.5% of GDP, have contributed less than 2% of all the country's domestic investment.

Most of the domestic savings is derived from corporate cash flow and from the large investment funds (superannuation, life savings, etc.) which are themselves a reflection of the skewed income distribution of the racially segregated society. Very little comes from other private personal savings, and as we have seen its proportion has been falling, a fact which reflects the high rates of inflation and rising levels of personal taxation. Also a reflection of the effects of apartheid, is the fact that a very great deal of the domestic investment from 1975 to 1980 went into the parastatal corporations - transport, electricity generation and supply, telecommunications, armaments production, oil substitutes - where the economy was either vulnerable to the effects of sanctions (if they should prove successful), or responding to the internal political (rather than economic) imperatives of apartheid. The strengthening of South Africa's infrastructure in this way has two contradictory consequences. On the one hand, by the misallocation of resources which it represents, it undermines and weakens the long-term prospects for efficiency and growth, thereby weakening apartheid. On the other, it provides short- and medium-term benefits which equip the regime better to resist the effects of world opposition to its policies.

From 1980, however, South Africa did start to borrow more from the international financial community. Between 1980 and the end of 1984, South Africa's total external debt, measured in US dollars, went up by 50% from $16.9 billion to $24.3 billion. If we think of the debt in local currency (Rand) terms, which is how it is seen inside South Africa, the growth in external debt looks rather more alarming. Because of the devaluation of the Rand, which began in 1981 and accelerated sharply in the second half of 1984, South Africa's external debt almost doubled in Rand terms between 1980 and 1982 (from R12.6 billion to R24.3 billion), and then doubled again in the two subsequent years to the end of 1984, when it stood at R48.2 billion.

The effects of devaluation were also reflected in the rise of external debt as a proportion of Gross Domestic Product, where there was an increase from 20.3% at the end of 1980 to 45.7% by the end of 1984.

Of this increase in borrowing, most was accounted for by the private sector, and much of it took the form of short-term borrowing – that is shorter than two years, and often as short as thirty to ninety days. By 1984 the proportion of South Africa's external debt that would mature within twelve months had risen to 65%, where it had stood at only 52% four years earlier.

South Africa was, of course, not alone in experiencing this development. The shift towards a reliance on private, shorter-term debt was a common feature internationally at this time, and in South Africa's case it took the form of a much greater reliance on supplier credits and short-term inter-bank borrowing. This trend was somewhat more marked in South Africa than elsewhere, however, and it had the effect of greatly increasing the country's vulnerability to any sudden financial difficulties.

The reasons for the change in posture towards a greater proportion of foreign short-term borrowing are fairly complex, but they are worth understanding because they illustrate further the extent to which South Africa's economic position is a product of the social policy goals summarised in apartheid. For a start, foreign funding appeared more attractive to South African borrowers because of relatively high domestic interest rates, themselves a consequence of attempts to hold down the rate of inflation. From mid-1983 to late 1985 real interest rates were positive, and actually exceeded 10% during 1984. Secondly, outside South Africa a move to ban lending to the South African government and its agencies was gathering pace. Increasingly the private sector was the only sector with access to foreign loans. There seems also to have been a growing desire among lenders for the sort of anonymity which is offered by inter-bank loans. It is hard, if not impossible, to tell where a loan originated if it occurs by a bank-to-bank transaction in which the apparent final lender can claim, truthfully, that it is merely the facilitator and not the lender. Simultaneously, there was a growing desire by lenders to limit their exposure over the medium and longer term because of what they perceived as political risks. One large London bank and another in New York began systematically to reduce their long- and medium-term exposure in South Africa at the end of 1983. Most lenders began to indicate that they preferred a short-term commitment, and started also to lay off their risks wherever this was possible. The trend towards short-term borrowing was exacerbated by South Africa's exchange control regulations which made early repayment of long-term debt difficult. As the Rand was in a period of erratic decline, long-term borrowers were locked into significant exchange risks, while short-term borrowers had more flexibility to manage these risks.

These developments illustrate the extent to which financial considerations affecting the South African economy are driven in some substantial degree by political considerations. Nor is this a recent development. Political events, and the perceptions of and about them by people who work in or through the international financial system, have had a significant impact on financial flows to South Africa since the early 1960s. The state of emergency that was imposed in the wake of the killings at Sharpeville in 1960 precipitated a surge of capital outflow and a fall in South Africa's reserves of foreign exchange and gold. Fears among investors that black opposition might now become black revolution meant that confidence returned only slowly, and was probably never fully re-established. Certainly by the early 1970s, the pressures from anti-apartheid movements in the West, and initiatives in the international forum of the United Nations, were making it increasingly difficult for governments or banks to continue to treat South Africa as a 'normal' member of the international community. In 1974 the Swiss announced that they were to restrict lending to South Africa by imposing an annual aggregate limit (or cap) of 250 million Swiss francs on all medium- and long-term loans to South African borrowers. The limit was raised to 300 million Swiss francs in 1980. According to their own figures (see Table 4.1), medium- and long-term Swiss lending to South Africa, though it reached the level of the cap in 1981, 1983 and 1984, has been considerably reduced since, and is fairly eloquent testimony of the impact that the events of 1985 have had on international financial market attitudes towards South Africa.

Table 4.1   Swiss Loans to South Africa, 1981–88 (Swiss francs millions)

Year	Amount
1981	301
1982	215
1983	300
1984	300
1985	83
1986	38
1987	52
1988	115

Both inside and outside banking circles, however, the view persists that it is the Swiss who are either actually now helping South Africa to overcome whatever difficulties it has with international financial markets, or may be about to do so. We can only say that our own inquiries have produced no evidence to support such a view.

Certainly Switzerland was ahead of international responses when it first imposed its cap in 1974. Close behind it came the Midland Bank in the United Kingdom, which ceased lending to the South African government or its agencies in 1975, moved to restrict all new loans to South African borrowers to finance trade with the United Kingdom in 1977, and closed its representative office in South Africa in 1978.

By this time the hideous events of the Soweto uprising and its repression of 1976 had once again undermined international financial confidence. Dutch commercial banks agreed to discontinue all commercial lending to the South African government in that year. A year later a number of large United Sates banks ceased lending to the government of South Africa or its agencies. In 1978 the Danish government terminated all official export credits, guarantees and insurance of Danish exports to South Africa. (In trade finance this is the crucial move. Without official government insurance provision, most commercial banks are reluctant to provide trade credits.) In 1979 Eximbank of the United States stopped making loans to the South African government and parastatals, and restricted its export credit facilities to those firms in the private sector that were applying the Sullivan code of principles. From the late 1970s onwards city and state legislatures in the United States (those with large and electorally significant black populations) began to sell their shareholdings in companies either in or doing business with South Africa and to withdraw business from banks known to be lending to South African entities. This local and state government response gathered some pace in the early 1980s, with New York's decision to go down this path in early 1985 one of the key developments that sparked decisions of the major New York banks later in the year.

These institutional responses apart, the Soweto events were also followed by net divestment of South African equities (the share market and other types of investment opportunity) which continued until 1982, and by annual debt outflows until 1981. After these events South Africa's relationship with the international financial community was reported by South African authorities to have returned to normal, but the pattern of both lending and borrowing thereafter, as we have seen, was fairly unusual in the degree of emphasis that it placed on short-term instruments. It was this development which made the South African financial system particularly vulnerable to any further loss of confidence. Moreover, it occurred, of course, in a context in which anti-apartheid activists outside South Africa had significantly augmented their campaigns for positive action against the regime. They worked to mobilise bank shareholders and workers, governments and international bodies, to oppose bank dealings with South Africa, and in particular with its government and other public bodies. As a sociological aside, it is worth reporting that many senior managers in the commercial banking sector in the West are practising Christians by conviction, and that the pressure of church groups has not been lost on them. Many seem profoundly cross-pressured by the commitments that they feel to purely ethical considerations on the one hand and the obligations of business on the other.

These developments must be kept in proportion, however. Significant as the international setting had become, and unusual as South Africa's position as an international borrower may have looked, the fact is that its international debt, in strictly economic terms, ought not to have been a problem. Table 4.2 sets out the figures for South Africa's gross external debt as a proportion of GDP over the years 1983 to 1987 inclusive, in comparison with a number of other countries.

What this table shows is that by international standards South Africa's external debt position was relatively healthy. Even in its worst recent year (1985) the ratio of debt to GDP in South Africa was less than half what it was in Denmark, and

Table 4.2   Gross External Debt as a Percentage of GDP, 1983–87

	South Africa	Canada	Australia	New Zealand	South Korea	Sweden	Denmark
1983	29.6	36.0	23.8	51.9	54.2	47.4	63.8
1984	34.6	36.0	24.2	59.0	54.1	45.0	70.0
1985	43.6	37.9	35.0	70.8	60.5	53.0	97.6
1986	36.9	41.4	42.5	78.2	52.9	47.8	88.7
1987	28.0	38.6	41.3	70.1	39.6	47.3	96.6

Source: Gross external debt statistics: Morgan international data.
GDP statistics: IMF international financial statistics.

less than two-thirds that of New Zealand. By 1987 the ratio was lower in South Africa than in any other of the countries shown here. What changed everything was not the economics of international finance but the politics of apartheid.

The passage of the constitutional changes in 1983, followed by the elections in 1984, explained and discussed in chapter two, provoked a renewed state of tension. Paradoxically for the regime, its attempt to expand its base of legitimacy actually served to highlight its illegitimacy by the continued and explicit exclusion of the black African population from any form of participation in national political life.

Riots and disorder broke out; the army was brought in to restore order, provoking further protest at and reaction against its repressive methods. The upsurge in violence, instability and unrest naturally took its toll on international financial confidence, as well as raising public pressures for some sort of response from the West. These reactions were also surely augmented by the extent to which the events were given the prominence they deserved in Western media.

Some evidence for this lies in the fact that in the twelve months to July 1985, seven states and twenty-five cities in the United States acted to move their business and investments away from companies and banks with South African connections, thereby joining the five states and twelve cities that had already done so over the previous four years.

The loss of confidence in general, however, was most clearly shown in the devaluation of the Rand, which lost a third of

its value in the year from June 1984 to June 1985 and, from the
third quarter of 1984 onwards, of the beginning of the outflow
of capital, both equity and debt, which has continued to this
day (see Table 3.9). Behind these statistics lies the reality of hard
business decisions being made in boardrooms across the
Western world. One large British bank reviewed its exposure
to South Africa in early 1985, and in response to all the
conditions outlined above decided to cease making new loans
to South African entities, and to get its then current exposure
down below a new, and lower, lending limit. Another British
bank took the decision in April to stop all new lending, and
there were reports of other banks, mostly with rather lower
exposure, shortening three-month securities to thirty days and
demanding wider spreads on inter-bank loans.

Interest rates on inter-bank loans are set by what is known
as LIBOR – London Inter-Bank Offer Rates – which are the
rates charged by London banks for lending to other banks. The
rates vary according to the length of period of the loan and
the currency in which it is denominated. The spread is the
difference between the LIBOR and the rate charged a particular
borrower. An alternative phrase might be 'higher interest rate
differentials'.

The social turmoil in South Africa continued unabated, and
on 20 July 1985 the government imposed the first of what were
to become four more or less continuous states of emergency.
This move, with its elements of increased repressive force,
limitations on media coverage and introduction of arrest and
detention without trial, served to bring international political
opposition to the regime, and financial nervousness about the
consequences of the unrest, to a point of great tension.

Events involving such a significant degree of turmoil, and
as much momentum, have a direct impact on international
financial opinion. The London *Sunday Times* reported (28 July
1985) that Frost Sullivan, the New York political risk consultants, had downgraded South Africa from among one of the
safest economies to the level of the higher-risk Third World
countries, a report which no doubt made up in impact for what

it lacked in subtlety. Shortly afterwards, Laurent Fabius, the French Prime Minister, announced government measures banning all new investment in South Africa by French commercial houses, and initiatives were started in the United Sates, the European Community, the Commonwealth, and the Nordic Council for the intensification of trade and other measures against South Africa.

In this context international financial markets responded further. Industrial and mining stocks on the South African exchange fell sharply as investors withdrew. R11 billion was wiped off the value of shares on the Johannesburg stock exchange in a week of trading at the end of July in what brokers described as a 'bloodbath' (Hirsch 1989, 5). The fact that South African institutions were scheduled to repay US$4 billion of short-term debt at the end of August, and that this sum was more than two and half times greater than the official reserves, became a matter of public comment and speculation, a fact which in turn put pressure on the forward market as debtors tried to sell Rand in order to cover themselves against the possibility of the debts not being renegotiated and their being forced to repay in United States dollars.

In an attempt to counter these developments the South African Reserve Bank cut its discount rate by 1.75%, the intention being to dispel the fear of liquidity shortages and to bolster market confidence. The effect, however, in the context of South Africa's continuing high rate of inflation (then still running at 16% in the wake of the 1984 commodity boom), and continuing depreciation of the Rand, was further to unsettle international confidence.

On the last day of July the *New York Times* reported that Chase Manhattan, with over US$600 million in outstanding loans to South Africa a substantial, but by no means the biggest creditor, had decided to refuse to roll over short-term credit and to freeze all agreed but unused credit lines to South African entities. Other American banks, though privately deeply critical of the decision by Chase, none the less moved to do the same. In mid-August Barclays Bank in London announced that it was going to reduce its South African interests, and news of the changes in lending policy already adopted by other British commercial banks seeped into the public arena. It began to appear as though what financial sector watchers call the 'herd instinct' was about to take over, and that financial institutions would begin to compete, not to stay in, but to get out of the South African market.

This was the setting in which the South African President, P. W. Botha, was to make a major policy speech in Durban on 15 August. The importance of this speech had been trailed by South Africa's Foreign Minister, Pik Botha, at a meeting in Vienna in early August with the American National Security Adviser Robert McFarlane, and according to the BBC's correspondent in South Africa (Leach 1986, 178) the news media had been briefed in advance that P. W. Botha would be announcing major new initiatives for the reform of apartheid. In the event, the speech, which was billed in advance as 'the Rubicon speech', contained no new substantive proposals, but the expectations that it aroused in anticipation produced a reaction in disappointment. The Rand came under further pressure, losing 20% of its value on 16 August and dropping to a new low of 35 cents. At this time one of the five South African commercial banks, finding itself unable to meet its forward commitments to supply foreign currency, went to the Reserve Bank for support. The SARB provided the funds to purchase the required foreign exchange, but the two American clearing banks with the responsibility for the transactions, instead of supplying the currency, seized the funds as repayments for outstanding loans. On 27 August, with the Rand at an historic all-time low of under 33 cents, and with numerous foreign companies repatriating as much as they could of past undistributed profits and thereby exacerbating the flight of capital, the gravity of the country's liquidity crisis, long recognised by the government, finally forced them to intervene. The stock and foreign exchange markets were closed until 2 September, and on 28 August the Governor of the SARB, Dr Gerhard de

Kock, left South Africa to visit London, Washington and New York, in search of support from the Bank of England, the Federal Reserve Bank, the International Monetary Fund and leading commercial banks.

The South African authorities have said that the purpose of his trip was to explain the measures that his government planned to take to stabilise the situation, but the real purpose seems to have been to seek support for moves to roll over short-term credits. This support was declined. It is also believed that he tried to get the Bank of England and the Federal Reserve to intervene with the Bank of International Settlements (BIS) for bridging support, but that the two central banks indicated that in the absence, and impossibility, of South Africa securing an arrangement with the IMF, a quorum in the BIS in favour of bridging support would hardly be forthcoming.

Deprived of international assistance, and with no other realistic alternatives, South Africa's Finance Minister du Plessis announced, on 1 September, a unilateral moratorium for four months on all principal repayments for all commercial bank debt, including short-term inter-bank loans. A dual exchange-rate system was reintroduced, with almost all capital transactions required to take place at the financial rather than the commercial Rand exchange rate. (The nature and effects of the dual exchange rate are explained in chapter five.)

The moratorium applied to about US$13.6 billion, or 60% of all outstanding debts, and was applied only to debts owing to commercial banks. All public bonds, debts guaranteed by governments and outstanding debts to international financial institutions (mainly the IMF) were excluded from the 'net'. The moratorium applied only to repayments, and not to the payment of interest which, pending negotiation of a new repayment schedule, was set at ¼% above LIBOR. In nominating a ¼% loading over LIBOR, the South African government was effectively conceding to lenders some compensation for the moratorium.

Worldwide there were approximately 250 banks caught with loans inside the 'net'. Most of them resented the fact that they were being treated in this way, both because there was other debt outside the 'net' which was to be repaid on time, and because they believed that all banks were being punished for what they regarded as the precipitate action of Chase and a few others.

Public bonds are thought to have been excluded from the moratorium for a number of reasons: the difficulty of renegotiating a schedule with the numerous holders; the risks of litigation (which were thought to be higher than for bank loans) coupled with the danger of being forced to make a formal declaration of default; the bad publicity that might flow from appearing to endanger the life savings of 'widows and orphans' (investment houses often having sizeable elements of these sorts of securities in their portfolios), and the desire to reward (or at least not punish) the European financial communities, who were the main holders of these sorts of securities and who were thought not to have participated in the 'panic' of July and August.

By far the greatest slice of debt not touched by the moratorium was owed to foreign government export credit agencies, however, and of this sum (approximately US$7.25 billion) about 90%, or US$ 6.5 billion, represented outstanding export trade credit finance owed to British, German and French government trade agencies. The South Africans were thought anxious to preserve access to this source of finance and to maintain good relations (in so far as this was still possible) with the governments of major trading partners. A similar motivation almost certainly governed the decision to exclude from the 'net' repayments owed to the IMF, with whom South Africa certainly wanted to continue to be a 'member in good standing' at a time when some members were actively contemplating moves to have it expelled.

Despite these attempts at rewarding some and not penalising others, the high-wire act could not disguise the fact that, in the terms and operating assumptions of international capital markets, South Africa had placed itself in the category of a problem debtor subject to rescheduling. Normal relations with international financial institutions would not be possible until or unless South Africa could shed this label. This objective thus became the principal aim of South African policy, and dictated that the government would seek to take a conciliatory approach in whatever discussions would now take place with the financial institutions whose loans had been caught in the 'net' (Harris 1986, *passim*).

As international bankers are often at pains to point out, there is not a great deal that can be done by them, at least in the short term, when a debtor defaults on its obligations. In theory a debtor's assets can be seized, but in practice this is almost always impossible. A bank that lends money to, say, a state-owned enterprise, has a contract with that enterprise and not with the government or some other enterprise. It cannot seize airliners or gold deposits or real estate that belongs to some other entity or agency of the government.

A little leverage might be exercised, although again largely in theory, by threatening to refuse to make trade credits available to the country concerned, but once again the difficulties here are very great. Most banks issue letters of credit for trade purposes in the interests of businesses and firms in their own countries, and since these are generally companies that have been valued clients of the banks, often for long periods of time, it would be poor and imprudent business to withdraw the service. The clients would just go elsewhere anyway.

None the less, immediately in the wake of the standstill, and while awaiting proposals from the South Africans on how they hoped to handle their difficulties, South African importers were largely being denied normal ninety-day credit terms and were having to pay cash with their orders.

A third and most obvious difficulty that the banks have in dealing with South Africa is that they are required to operate within the laws of the countries in which they are registered, and in most instances this involves them in meeting the obligation of ensuring that their shareholders' interests are protected. When a debtor defaults through government intervention in a foreign country, most banks interpret their primary obligation as trying to ensure the evolution of a situation in which, by one means or another, they can get their money back. The law requires them to do it. The political and economic circumstances in this instance meant that South Africa was in the short term, at least apparently (though we shall see in due course how far this is an appearance rather than a reality) able to dictate terms.

None the less, because of the unusual political circumstances (there was still turmoil on the streets of the black townships) the banks were not prepared to sit down with South African negotiators to work out a mutually satisfactory arrangement. Eventually, and instead, the South Africans persuaded Dr Fritz Leutwiler, formerly Chairman of the Bank for International Settlements, and a former Governor of the Swiss Central Bank, to act as an independent 'arbitrator' in devising a plan under which the repayment of debt caught inside the 'net' could be resumed. In this role, to which he appears to have been persuaded on the basis of a commitment by the South African government to undertake reform, Dr Leutwiler acted as intermediary between a South African Standstill Co-ordinating Committee, chaired by Dr Chris Stals, and representatives of the thirty largest creditor banks whose outstanding loans accounted for 70% of all the debt caught inside the 'net'.

The Standstill Co-ordinating Committee's main objectives were to avoid litigation and the possible seizure of South African assets abroad – a generally illusory danger, as we have seen. Secondly, they were to get normal trade finance facilities restored, and thirdly to return to normal relations with the international financial community as quickly as possible.

In pursuit of these objectives their first proposal was that the US$13.6 billion of short-term debt should be converted into medium-term debt, with slightly increased margins of interest and repayments of principal to begin in 1990. These proposals were turned down by the banks. Many had thirty- to ninety-day inter-bank credit lines caught in the 'net', and were not prepared to see them turned into multi-year loans. Some wanted higher rates of interest. They all said that they wanted to see some commitment to political reform.

Dr Leutwiler reported back to his South African clients on 10 December, and in response to the fact that the search for an agreement appeared deadlocked, they extended their moratorium for a further three months to 31 March 1986. Then, apparently as a gesture in the direction of the political reforms that the banks had indicated were a precondition for settlement, P. W. Botha, in a speech on 31 January 1986, indicated that the government planned the abolition of influx control by the end of June, and the involvement of black communities in decision-making.

The banks were informed of these intentions in advance, and they paved the way for Dr Leutwiler to meet the banks' representatives in London during February 1986. On this occasion he presented a package the main features of which were:
• an interim settlement until 30 June 1987 (that is fifteen months duration)
• an increase of 1% in the interest payable
• an immediate principal repayment of 5% on those debts originally maturing before the end of March 1986
• a 5% principal repayment on the original maturity date of all other debt caught in the 'net'.
A further round of negotiations would then be held in the first half of 1987 to decide what to do next. Leutwiler apparently stressed that he believed the South African offer of reform to be in good faith, but that he also believed that the offer he was now making to the banks was the best that they would get. If it was unacceptable to them, then he would resign.

The banks had really no choice but to accept, a fact that was emphasised by the treatment meted out to the 230 or so smaller creditors who learned of the deal in a letter which noted that a telex acknowledging receipt would be regarded as an acceptance. Most banks caught in the process took the view that not accepting would make little difference, since the South African authorities would simply treat them as though they had accepted anyway. But when a few of the small creditor banks in the United States (and possibly Japan) declined to accept, and moved to declare their South African loans non-performing, the larger creditors intervened to purchase the smaller debts. This was because most of these kinds of loans have cross-default clauses in the contracts, which mean that if one client defaults then all other creditors will be compelled to move simultaneously to protect their own legal position with respect to their own debtors. The result, in this instance, would have been literally hundreds of court cases involving hundreds of creditors and hundreds of their clients, all making court submissions and all engaged in a competitive race to attach assets. The consequences in legal terms would, in the case of South African debt in 1985, probably have been greater than they were at the collapse of the London tin market.

There was some opinion voiced in anti-apartheid circles that the banks had been wrong to settle with the Standstill Co-ordinating Committee, and that by doing so they had removed the pressure which the financial crisis was imposing on the South African regime. The banks take the view, however, that they had no option. They believed that the Leutwiler Agreement, with its short duration, political commitments, and clear airing of their dissatisfaction, maintained the pressure on the government of South Africa and, indeed, went as far as it was possible to go without the sustained pressure forcing South Africa to default altogether, and repudiate the debt. What the consequences of repudiation might be is a subject to which we return in chapter eight.

There was then a ten-month breathing space during which the South African Public Investment Commission (PIC) which was, technically, now the holder of the rolled over debts, met the repayment obligations (both interest and principal) that the Leutwiler Agreement required. At the beginning of 1987, with the interim arrangement due to expire at the end of June, a new round of meetings was organised. This time the main creditors had formed what they called a Technical Committee to co-ordinate their approach. The committee consisted of representatives of three United Kingdom banks (Barclays, NatWest and Standard Chartered), three Swiss banks (Credit Suisse, Union Bank of Switzerland and the Swiss Banking Corporation), three German banks (Dresdner, Commerzbank and Deutschesbank), and three American banks (Citicorp, Manufacturers Hanover Trust and Morgan Guaranty). Two French banks (Indo-Suez and Credit Lyonnais) joined slightly later. For the South African regime negotiations were handled directly by Dr Stals, who had now become Director General of Finance. He met European banking representatives in London in January, American bankers in New York in February, and the Technical Committee, to whom he formally put his proposals, in March.

The effects of a diminution in international publicity for the ugly events inside South Africa, and the relative success of the mass arrests as a strategy for reducing street violence and turmoil, were reflected in the fact that the bankers no longer felt the same inhibitions about talking directly to representatives of the regime. Nor did Dr Stals find it either necessary or expedient to raise the issue of political reforms, despite the fact that, although the Pass Laws had been abolished, none of the other proposals put forward by P. W. Botha a year earlier had been acted upon. Overall, these second negotiations for an interim arrangement appear to have been very much smoother than the first, itself an indication of the degree to which the banks were now coming to terms with the fact that the only way they were likely to get their money back was to hope for some stability in South Africa while pressing for the best repayment schedule that they could get.

The offer that was finally agreed by the Technical Committee, and circulated by Dr Stals to all the creditors for their formal acceptance, was presented as an extension of the March 1986 arrangements. In fact it took the form of a slowing of repayments. The new period of rescheduling was thirty-six months, to the end of June 1990, with a further 13% of the outstanding capital to be repaid over that period: 3% on 15 July 1987, 2% on 15 December 1987 and 15 June 1988 and 1.5% on

15 December 1988, 15 June and 15 December 1989, and 15 June 1990. The reasons for this slow-down are difficult to understand (though we attempt an explanation in chapter eight) because at the time there had been some publicity for the view that repayments might increase in the light of an improvement in the price of gold.

As far as interest payments were concerned, the same favourable terms as had been offered under the first interim agreement were to be continued.

What was really new in the second agreement, however, was an offer for the holders of debt caught in the 'net' to get free of it through one of two exit options. The first, which has become known as the ten-year option, proposed that creditors convert their debt to long-term credits for maturity in 1997. These credits would receive the same treatment as all debts caught in the 'net' until June 1990, after which there would be a two-year moratorium on payments, followed by ten half-yearly payments of capital until 1997. Interest over the last seven years (that is after 1990) would be payable at a 'reasonable rate' to be negotiated between the individual lender and the South African borrower.

The second exit option offered creditors the right to use their claims to purchase equities inside South Africa (in other words, a creditor could convert its debt into cash inside South Africa and invest the proceeds on the stock market). The creditor would then be free to sell the equities and repatriate the proceeds, but only at the financial Rand rate, which would involve a discount, or loss, of perhaps as much as 25% to 40%. (See chapter five for an explanation of the dual exchange rate system.)

These exit option proposals lay on the table in 1987. Given that the first of them would not take effect until 1990 anyway, banks had a period for reflection. Given that the second of them involved a sizeable write-down in the capital investment, hardly anyone was inclined to accept. The rest of the package, however, was accepted by the banks, and news of this acceptance was received in the South African financial and business media as very bullish news. It was described as indicating 'a major shift in the perceptions and attitudes towards South Africa of some of the world's biggest and most influential banks' and as 'taking the sting out of the most damaging sanction yet' (Wilson 1987, 110). The fact that the agreement covered three years was seen as giving South Africa the time to get its economy in order, and to attempt, by exhortation, PR and influence (mostly out of the public eye) to attract new foreign investment into the country.

A certain amount has been written and said in criticism of the banks for coming to the second interim agreement. It is worth while trying to understand, in the light of this criticism, exactly how the current arrangements for the rescheduling work, and why it is that the various participants have only very limited room for manoeuvre.

Most of the debt caught inside the 'net' consists of loans made by foreign banks to various banks and other private entities inside South Africa. These borrowers are prohibited from making repayments, either of interest or of principal, in excess of those provided for in the accord, by provisions in the South African Currency and Exchanges Act.

The only room for variation, either for lenders or for borrowers, is provided for in three provisions. First, they may agree to roll over or extend the loan at a mutually agreed interest rate provided that this is not more than 1% higher than the rate payable before the moratorium. Second, by mutual agreement, they may have a third party take over the debt within the same interest rate limit. Third, the borrower could make repayments according to the original schedule, but these would be deposited in a special account with the PIC where they would earn interest at a margin $7/8\%$ above the relevant LIBOR rate. These funds are then invested in South African government securities, except that the lender may at any time arrange to lend the money to some other private sector entity if it prefers, provided always that the interest rate is not higher than the prescribed ceiling.

The effect of these provisions is to ensure that the foreign loans are effectively held in captivity for the duration of the moratorium. Funds accumulating in PIC accounts and used for investment in government securities are effectively loans to the South African government. Many banks are unwilling to lend to the regime, which is further inducement for them to accept the slightly higher interest rates that they can acquire by relending the funds to other private sector clients, which is their only alternative. By doing so, however, they have to accept management costs involved in administering their funds and, which is of more interest to the South African regime, they have to sustain banker–client relations with private sector entities (companies, corporations, etc.) to whom they lend the money, thereby keeping a presence in the infrastructure of South African business and commerce. To do this, some banks have to maintain representative offices in South Africa (this is the case with seven West German banks, four French banks and three major Swiss banks), while others either have to commit themselves to regular visits, or have to work through correspondent banks. Three of the formerly largest banking presences in South Africa, Barclays, Standard Chartered and Citicorp, have all disinvested since 1985, but still have the task of ensuring the proper management of the funds which, looked at in a slightly different light, have really been confiscated by the South African authorities for their own purposes. None the less, as the imprisoned funds are redeployed under the Stals Agreement the impression is unfortunately created that major foreign banks are engaging in new lending. This is not true, but it serves the interests of the South African regime to allow this to appear to be the case, just as it also serves their interest to have major foreign financial institutions compelled (by the fact that they have money invested in them) to take an interest in the future prosperity of various South African companies and firms.

These aspects of the agreement have weighed heavily on all the participants in the two years since the second rescheduling came into force in 1987. They now form the principal focus of all the thinking that is taking place in the approach to the end of the interim agreement in June 1990. Of the US$13.6 billion caught in the 'net' in 1985, only 18% will have been repaid by the time the agreement runs out. Approximately US$12 billion still remains due. In addition to this, approximately another US$2 billion in bonds also fall due for repayment in 1990. Will the South Africans be able to pay?

This question is the subject of lively debate in financial circles. Over the four years since 1985 the regime has met all its repayments inside the 'net', and also continued to service and to repay debts that were left outside the 'net' (including its debt to the IMF). For the past four years South Africa has run surpluses on its current account (see chapter three) but these surpluses continue to be heavily influenced by gold sales, and the price of gold has been drifting slowly downwards (see chapter seven). The effects of this are registered in the official reserves, which at the end of 1988 stood at R4.9 billion, the lowest level since 1986 and far too low, if they were to continue at this level until June 1990, to enable the government even to contemplate paying off the debt outstanding to foreign financial institutions. They will be forced to renegotiate.

Recognising this fact, the South African authorities appear to have put a lot of effort into trying to persuade their foreign creditors to accept the ten-year option that formed part of the Stals accord. Their objective appears to have been to try to get US$5 billion of the debt rolled over into this kind of long-term loan, presumably on the assumption that with no principal repayments on this part of the debt to fund for the two years from 1990 to 1992 they would be able to accelerate the repayment of those loans that were not rolled over in this way. Certainly some banks have been playing their hands very close to their chests about whether or not they are prepared to accept the ten-year option, partly because the more who do accept the offer, the faster the remainder can expect to get their money out. Others, such as one major British bank, have decided to divide their debt and put half into the long-term option and keep the other half for a new interim agreement. Another, Citicorp, having made its decision to accept the ten-year option, has gone public, and said as much. It is still too early to know exactly how many international banks with money caught in the 'net' will agree to roll over their loans until 1997, but preliminary estimates that we have been able to make suggest that some US$4 billion (or one-third of what is outstanding) will be rescheduled in this way.

Both the South African regime and the critics of apartheid will regard this development as indicating support from international banks. This perception is probably false, however. One major international banker expressed it to us in the following way: that the 1997 option offered them an opportunity to say once and for all that they were done with South Africa; that they did not even wish to be involved in renegotiating short-term roll-overs; that it was impossible inside South Africa to provide the kind of professional environment that was essential to the recruitment and maintainance of first-rate personnel; that in the absence of thorough-going reform of the political and social arrangements the prospects for the country were very poor, and that the 1997 option at least offered the prospect, after 1992, of getting their money back. Far from providing support for apartheid, this bank saw the decision to take the long-term option as a clear signal that they would have no more to do with the country.

In a curious way, and as a consequence of the multilateral bargaining situation in which the participants find themselves, those contemplating the short-term option see similar advantages. As long as enough of the others go for the long term, then those staying short will get out faster. The line up so far suggests that German, Swiss and French banks will stick to the short-term renegotiations, while British banks will split their loans between the two, and American banks will prefer the ten-year option.

The South African authorities are expected to start negotiations with individual creditors very shortly. At the beginning of 1990 they will then once again meet the Technical Committee to see if a common approach is acceptable. Unity on the Technical Committee is likely to be rather harder to get this time around. Citicorp, having already decided to take the ten-year option, will no longer be a member. The South African negotiators, who will know in advance which of the other members have already decided to accept the long-term option and in what proportions, will have a much stronger bargaining hand. The members of the Technical Committee take the view that they have two common objectives: to protect the interests of all the smaller creditors who are not part of the negotiations, but who will be compelled to accept whatever agreement is finally adopted, and to have their money returned to them as quickly as possible. Beyond that, they admit that they are relatively powerless to influence whatever the South African authorities decide to offer. We were also left with the impression that in this third round of negotiations the Technical Committee would be rather more divided against itself over the issue of political risk and South Africa's general credit-worthiness. Some bankers clearly take the view that there is nothing fundamentally wrong with the South African economy, and that it offers good investment opportunities that banks ought to be free to pursue once the moratorium has been disposed of. Others, perhaps those with a rather stronger analytical framework for assessing risk in the context of the evolving structure of South Africa's economy, regard the prospects as very gloomy.

None, however, is particularly free to choose one way or the other. Most international financial institutions are under either voluntary restraint or compulsory prohibition on any further medium- or long-term lending to South Africa. We examine and explain these arrangements in chapter six where we look at South Africa's problem with capital flows in general. For now, however, it is appropriate to point out that in all countries commercial bank lending activities are subject to regulation, and that in many of the advanced countries this regulation is undertaken by the central bank itself. One important element in the regulations is to ensure that banks, when making loans, have made adequate provision against the possibility of losses. The more a borrowing country is regarded as being a risk, the higher the level of financial provision that has to be made against any loan. The amount of the provision varies from country to country, but in the United Kingdom banks follow a formula known as the Bank of England matrix. The matrix provides a method, largely based on the historic performance of a country in meeting its debt obligations, for assessing the level of provisioning that is required if a new loan is to be advanced. This kind of regulator, when applied, has the effect of reducing the profitability of lending the higher a country 'scores' on the matrix. Rules regarding loan loss provisioning may, therefore, themselves constitute a disincentive to lending, particularly of the incremental type.

In Canada, for instance, where the provisioning rules are tight in connection with those countries that have had to reschedule debts, the disincentive to lending to South Africa is as great as that against lending to debt-distressed developing countries. In the Federal Republic of Germany the Bundesbank enforces provisioning requirements that are so strict as to rule out any lending to South African entities for longer than twelve months.

The role of central banks in this area is just another indicator of the complex set of forces that are at work in the arena of international financial links with South Africa. A full account of these forces would be incomplete without a more systematic treatment of the functions of central banks, and of the international banking institutions that now play such an important part in the world economy.

The International Monetary Fund (IMF) and the World Bank

South Africa is an original member of the World Bank, which it joined in 1945, and it has increased its subscriptions over the years both in quotas to the IMF and in capital to the World Bank, when required to do so.

There have been attempts to evict South Africa from both institutions. After the United Nations General Assembly voted to refuse South Africa further participation in its work in 1974, the Secretary-General wrote to the Managing Director of the IMF and the President of the World Bank, informing them of the decision and suggesting that they take similar action. The IMF did not reply. The World Bank replied by saying that it had its own articles of agreement, that only its board was responsible for their interpretation, and that it was not prepared to take the same action as the United Nations. In other words, though it agreed that it was a part of the UN system of international organisations, it did not regard itself as in any way obliged to follow decisions of the General Assembly in New York. It did say at the same time, however, that it would not be making any further loans to South Africa – though by 1974 it was questionable whether South Africa would have been entitled to any because of its level of economic development.

Formal expulsion from the two bodies was hardly necessary given the institutional setting in which South Africa found itself. The IMF and the World Bank are formally governed by boards of governors, which meet annually. Day-to-day operations are ensured by executive boards of directors, and the directors, with the exception of those representing the largest shareholder countries, represent constituencies of countries. South Africa used to be a member of constituencies in both institutions that included Australia and New Zealand. Both those countries indicated in 1974 that their voting group did not wish to continue to represent South Africa. Unable to find another group to which it could belong, South Africa was not able to participate in the election of executive directors and since then has ceased to be represented by any director on either board.

As a result South Africa's position at the IMF and the World Bank is much the same as it is at the United Nations. By virtue of its refusal to withdraw it has all the rights and obligations of the institution, but can play no part and has no say in its daily operations. It maintains an official in Washington as 'Principal Resident Representative to the IMF and the World Bank', but this person may participate only in board meetings

discussing South Africa, and may only attend as an observer
those meetings at which matters of direct relevance to South
Africa are discussed. In addition to being thus excluded from
discussion on the great range of world economic topics, South
Africa is also excluded from the important committees of
governors which meet twice a year for ministerial-level discussion of international economic policy issues. The only occa-
sions when South Africa can even appear to be taking part are
when its Minister of Finance, as his country's governor of the
two institutions, attends the annual meetings and has an
opportunity to speak in his turn. These meetings do not make
substantive decisions on the important matters of loans and
advances, however, and in recent years the South Africans
have been allotted meetings that are generally sparsely
attended. (Usually the very last slot in the late after-
noon/evening session immediately preceding the formal
dinner for governors.)

Under these circumstances it would appear more than a little
quixotic to press for South Africa's expulsion from either the
IMF or the World Bank, but there are institutional reasons that
would add to the difficulties as well. As with the UN, the
Articles of Agreement of the IMF and the World Bank reflect
the principle of universality of membership, though in the case
of the bank, membership is conditional on membership of the
IMF. Not all members of the UN belong to the IMF, but
membership is open to all countries which accept the obligations of membership. This open approach reflects in turn the
functional objectives of the two institutions: the promotion of
orderly financial arrangements for the purposes of encouraging
trade and economic growth and the promotion of economic
development in the Third World. Much of the thinking that
lay behind the Bretton Woods discussions out of which these
institutions were built emphasised the fact that the benefits
of membership would not necessarily accrue to each individual
country, but to the international community as a whole. In this
sense it is worth reflecting on the fact (unfortunately little
known to the general public) that the IMF's annual staff

mission under Article IV on the state of the South African economy and its prospects, is one of the most comprehensive sources of serious, intelligent and hard-nosed analysis of South Africa that is available to other countries. Black African (and other) states in the forefront of international opposition to apartheid could not hope to acquire these annual data or analyses from any other source. It is evidence of the unreal quality of perception about themselves and the international environment that one South African banker could be reported as saying (*Euromoney*, December 1986): 'The authorities [in South Africa] pay little attention to economic advice from the IMF technicians anyway'. If this is true, they are in a tiny minority. Most other governments and central banks find IMF reports on South Africa in the same league as the mongoose for hypnotic fascination.

Apart from the general benefits that accrue to the international community, of which any individual country is, of course, a member, the main direct benefit that members may derive from membership of the IMF is the opportunity to draw funds to meet international debt obligations at a time when external accounts are weak or in deficit, and reserves are low. In other words, the situation in which South Africa has found itself ever since 1985. South Africa has the same theoretical access to IMF resources as other member countries at its level of development. Under the rules a country may draw from the fund an amount equivalent to its quota (that is, the amount it has paid in) without first getting board approval, but this only constitutes drawing down to what is called its reserve position (the resources that it has itself contributed). Further drawings have to be approved by the Executive Board on the recommendation of the Managing Director, and where the drawing exceeds 125% of quota the fund requires that the borrower implement a fund-approved program of economic stabilisation measures. Whether its application puts it above or below the 125% level, when a country applies for a drawing the board requires that its staff carry out an assessment of the borrower's economic policies and performance.

South Africa has drawn funds down to its reserve position, and knows full well that it would get little comfort from an IMF analysis of its economic policies. When the IMF Executive Board discussed South Africa early in 1988 directors were critical of the extent to which the policies and practices of apartheid constituted a significant labour market rigidity, the effect of which was to reduce efficiency significantly. The implications of this criticism make it extremely unlikely that South Africa could approach the IMF for further drawing rights without adjusting its domestic economic stance by terminating the various labour regulations that derive from the practice of apartheid.

This is a fairly significant change from the recent past. In 1982 the IMF did provide South Africa with a Stand-By Arrangement, and with what is known as a compensatory financing facility. South Africa drew 159 million Special Drawing Rights (SDRs) under this arrangement. The final payments on this loan, which were made in 1987, represented part of the external debt that was not included in the moratorium of 1 September 1985.

However, by 1985 things had changed. South Africa did not apply for an IMF loan then because it would not have got one. The US Domestic Housing and International Recovery and Financial Stability Act of 1983 amended the Bretton Woods Agreement Act to require the United States Director of the IMF to vote against requests for use of fund resources by countries practising apartheid. Apartheid was seen to involve severe constraints on labour and capital mobility which contributed to balance of payments difficulties 'in direct contradiction of the goals of the IMF'. Therefore, unless the Treasury Secretary informed the relevant Congressional committees, at least twenty-one days in advance of any such program being considered by the Executive Board, that the proposed use of IMF resources would:

- directly reduce the severe constraints on labour and capital mobility
- directly reduce other labour and capital supply rigidities

- clearly benefit, economically, the majority of the people in the country concerned
- address a genuine balance of payments need which could not be met by recourse to private capital markets

then the Executive Director would be instructed to vote against the proposal.

While the other countries represented on the Executive Board of the IMF have not explicitly followed the United States lead, there is general acceptance that a proposal to lend to South Africa would not receive majority support from the board.

Themselves aware of the difficulty, the commercial banks did not insist that South Africa adopt an IMF program, knowing full well that it would refuse because of anticipating what the IMF's response would be. The SARB Governor, de Kock, said in a speech in Zurich (8 October 1987) that South Africa did not have the option of an IMF loan in 1985, and there were various reports that his acceptance of this fact followed private soundings of the fund and its major members that revealed that an approach would be unlikely to secure board approval.

Meanwhile, South Africa's potential right to draw from the fund has also been in decline. The right to draw down funds is calculated as a function of what is called its quota share. Quotas are allocated on the basis of a negotiated formula, the main components of which are its reserves, its share of world trade, its Gross Domestic Product, and its past (historic) quotas (this last being used in recognition of the international role that is played by some currencies). Quotas are negotiated from time to time in reviews – the Ninth Quota Review is taking place this year – and the strong likelihood is that South Africa's quota will decline, as it did in the Eighth Quota Review. Its share of world trade has fallen from 0.69% in 1982 to 0.48% in 1987, and informed opinion considers that South Africa's quota share could fall below 1% for the first time as a result.

Unlike the IMF, the World Bank is really a group of three organisations: the International Bank for Reconstruction and Development (IBRD), the International Development Association (IDA), and the International Finance Corporation (IFC). South Africa participates in all three, having 0.97% of the votes in the IBRD, 0.31% in the IDA and 0.7% in the IFC. In the past South Africa has received a number of project loans from the World Bank, all of them fully serviced and repaid, the last being discharged in 1976. There is no basis now for South Africa qualifying for loans again, however, even though its declining economic performance and the devaluation of the Rand have reduced per capita income to the level at which in theory it could apply to be reinstated as a potential borrower. The procedure for reinstatement includes a review of the country's broad economic policies, and South Africa would fail to meet the standards of such a review without far-reaching policy reforms.

South Africa does benefit a little from providing goods and services for projects supported by World Bank loans. Procurements of this kind were estimated to be worth about US$69 million in the 1987 financial year. The benefit flows, naturally, from South Africa's advantageous geographical position which makes it a competitive bidder for contracts on projects in neighbouring African countries. The current World Bank guidelines for procurement state:

firms of a member country or goods manufactured in a member country may be excluded if, as matter of law or official regulation, the Borrower's country prohibits commercial relations with that country, provided that the Bank is satisfied that such exclusion does not preclude effective competition for the supply of goods or works required.

Under this guideline it seems clear that the World Bank has recognised the right of borrowing countries to impose sanctions on procurement for projects.

South Africa joined both the IFC and the IDA when they were founded, in 1957 and 1960 respectively. However, South African companies are not eligible to borrow from the IFC. South Africa's contribution to the IDA (US$9.2 million in the most recent program, IDA VIII), as a proportion of GNP, is approximately the same as that of the US. A recent (1987) IDA credit of US$9.8 million to fund the engineering phase of a hydro scheme in Lesotho is of direct benefit to South Africa, which will be able to purchase water from the scheme. These purchases will eventually pay for the project, which will provide electrical power for Lesotho. This development is illustrative of a fact about southern Africa: that development work in the Southern African Development Co-ordination Conference (SADCC) countries, which the World Bank supports, can only with difficulty exclude the benefits of either participation or outcome also flowing to South Africa. This is one more reason why it is a matter of urgency for apartheid to be dismantled. The full participation of a democratic South Africa in the economic development of its region is a pressing necessity, and one that international financial institutions, private and public, would wholeheartedly support.

The Bank for International Settlements

There has been some speculation that South Africa might have been able to borrow from the Bank for International Settlements (BIS). The BIS was founded in 1930 to handle the administration of the German Government International Loan – part of the machinery for trying to deal with First World War reparations payments – but has evolved into an institution which performs trustee and banking services for central banks and provides a consultative forum for central bankers. The SARB is a member (which involves holding a small number of shares) and also a customer. The secrecy provisions of the BIS mean that there is little public information about the services that it provides for central banks, and it does not publish statistics about its assets in sufficient detail to enable us to make confident judgements about the loans that it advances. None the less, it is reasonable to assume that the SARB has funds on deposit with the BIS, that the BIS holds gold for South Africa, and that it occasionally executes purchase and sell orders of gold, currency, bonds and notes.

The only loans that the BIS might make available to the SARB would be short-term loans (with full collateral by gold) and bridging loans of the sort that it currently makes available to debtor or developing countries which have to meet certain payments in advance of drawing down stand-by credits from the IMF, or receiving World Bank loan disbursements. BIS bridging loans are guaranteed by the central banks of the major industrialised countries, are for short terms and are tied to an IMF program. All of these conditions make it impossible for South Africa to obtain this kind of support from the BIS.

So long as it is the policy of governments to continue to permit some trade with South Africa, foreign currency transactions will have to be permitted, and South Africa will have to be allowed to hold assets in foreign currencies. The foreign exchange reserves of South Africa, as with other countries, are managed by its central bank, the SARB, which would certainly invest in treasury bills and other government securities in the countries whose currencies are normally used for reserves and international payments. These investments may be made through another central bank or through a commercial bank. As is the practice of other indebted countries, the SARB almost certainly has substantial funds on deposit with those commercial banks from which its government has borrowed. Some might argue that this was bringing 'comfort' to South Africa, and ought to be stopped. It is hard to see that this is the case, or that it is possible. Provided that some large enough banking institution somewhere in the world is prepared to provide depositor and investor facilities to the SARB, then it doesn't make much difference that others do too. In any event, as far as the international commercial community is concerned, the knowledge that South Africa has reserves provides the confidence that its central bank will use them to off-set short-term fluctuations in receipts and payments. In other words, that it will continue to make orderly trade possible.

What would be more important to discover, at least from the point of view of not bringing financial comfort to South Africa, is whether any central banks have swap lines with South Africa, thereby permitting it to borrow under the line to support the Rand. We are not able to give a definitive answer to this question, though the collapse of the Rand in 1985 suggests that if they did exist they were inadequate to the task. Furthermore, it is the general practice of central banks to confine this practice to the major currencies in which international confidence necessarily has to reside. One would hardly describe the currency of South Africa, in its present political and economic disarray, as falling into this category.

CHAPTER FIVE

The Dual Exchange Rate System

South Africa has operated a dual exchange rate for all but two and a half years since 1961 when, in the wake of Sharpeville, it experienced a sudden outflow of capital. The arrangements that came into force then were maintained until 7 February 1983, when the government dispensed with them and went over to a single exchange rate as part of a general drive to try to liberalise and invigorate the economy. Its reintroduction on 2 September 1985, when the exchanges reopened after the August financial crisis, is, therefore, an admission of failure. The dual exchange rate is a direct response to the pressures exerted by the flight of capital. Just how serious this flight has been in recent years is set out in Table 5.1.

In his budget speech in 1988 the Minister of Finance foreshadowed the possibility that capital outflows would be reversed in 1988–89 on the basis of trade-related credits being available, and rising domestic interest rates. These circumstances would permit South African traders to substitute foreign credits for the domestic borrowing that they had relied on over the previous few years. In actual fact, as Table 5.1 shows, capital outflows intensified throughout 1988, producing an outcome more than twice as bad as the preceding year, and worse even than 1986 when the domestic political crisis was still threatening visible instability.

Table 5.1 Balance of Payments: Capital Account, 1980–88 (R millions)

	1980	1981	1982	1983	1984	1985	1986	1987	1988
Net long-term capital	-478	542	2 433	-238	2 563	-445	-3 060	-1 698	-1 052
Net short-term capital	-1 804	419	797	290	-1 772	-8 786	-3 037	-1 371	-5 611
Net capital movements	-2 282	961	3 230	52	791	-9 231	-6 097	-3 069	-6 663

Source: SARB Quarterly Bulletins.

As things stand, the regime invests considerable administrative effort in trying to stem the outflow of capital, and the
exchange rate system is an important part of the process. It
is, therefore, worth examining the dual exchange rate system
in some detail because the foreign exchange regulations
exercise a pervasive influence on the movements of capital into
and out of South Africa. They also contribute very greatly to
the pace and character of disinvestment, which we examine
in chapter six, and so are worth understanding at this point
in the development of our argument. The arrangements apply
not only to South Africa but also to currency transactions in
and out of Lesotho and Namibia, which are part of a monetary
union with South Africa, and, to all intents and purposes, are
completely captive to the South African economy as a whole.

A dual exchange rate system has a certain amount in
common with the artificial exchange rate systems operated by
communist regimes. The two tiers of the system are called the
commercial Rand and the financial Rand. Anyone applying for
permission to move money into or out of South Africa will pass
through one or other of the tiers, which are so organised as
to maximise the advantages of placing capital in South Africa,
and the costs of taking it out.

The commercial Rand exchange rate is the rate that you
would get for trading commodities with South Africa: all
imports and exports are paid for at this exchange rate. So too
are all invisibles, such as dividends, royalties and licence fees.
If you purchase equities on the South African stock market,
and they turn a profit, your dividends would be paid at the
commercial Rand exchange rate. Rock singers get their record
royalties at this rate, as do all those foreign companies that
receive fees for the licences that they hold over machinery, or
technical knowledge, or franchises of one kind or another. The
commercial Rand exchange rate is also the rate that would
apply to any commercial loan that was being made to a South
African entity. That is, if a South African company borrowed
capital from a foreign commercial source, both the capital sum
going into South Africa and the interest and principal repay-

ments going out to service it, would pass through the commercial Rand exchange rate.

This commercial Rand rate is quoted by the commercial banks according to supply and demand (that is it apparently floats) but in practice the rate is very much influenced by the SARB, which takes a continuous and interventionist interest in it. In economists' parlance it is a very dirty float indeed. SARB intervention, when it is direct, is usually in US dollars, and is usually directed at stabilising the rate of exchange. Since the beginning of the decade South Africa has been resigned to devaluation, but the SARB has sought, within the broad acceptance of this necessity, to bring the rate down in a controlled and orderly manner. It was the loss of control in August 1985 which resulted in the market being closed (which is the ultimate form of intervention) and the return to the dual exchange rate system (which gives more immediate impact to all interventionist decisions). Failure to generate substantial surpluses on the current account of the balance of payments also limits the SARB's ability to intervene in support of the currency.

In addition to direct support for the commercial Rand, the SARB also has some other powerful weapons for influencing the commercial Rand exchange rate.

Firstly, the entire output of the gold-mining industry has to be sold to the SARB within one month of production (i.e. no hoarding by the mining companies as a means of influencing prices). The SARB is then itself the agent for all international gold sales, gold swaps, and other international currency operations involving gold. (See chapter seven for a more detailed treatment of the gold market.) Since gold sales have a direct bearing on the size of South Africa's reserves, and since its reserves in turn have a direct bearing on international perceptions of the vitality of its economy and hence of its currency, control over gold is a useful instrument in commercial Rand exchange rate manipulation.

So too are the many regulatory controls which exist, and which permit the authorities a wide discretion in day-to-day economic activity. Import permits are required for many goods, and export permits for some. Payments of royalties and licence fees to foreigners all require approval by the Department of Trade and Industry as well as approval by the SARB. The timing of payments for imports and for services purchased overseas are strictly controlled under rules that permit the authorities wide discretion, and the remittance of foreign exchange earnings is also carefully monitored. All of these regulations permit indirect intervention in the exchange rate for the commercial Rand, and are employed for this purpose. The recent course of the exchange rate for the commercial Rand against the US dollar is set out in columns (1) and (2) of Table 5.2.

The lower tier of the exchange rate system is called the financial Rand. This is the rate of exchange that is applied to the following five broad categories of commercial activity:

(a) investments in South Africa by non-residents. This covers such economic activity as the purchasing of equities on the South African stock market, or the purchasing of bonds previously issued by, say, a South African local government or parastatal corporation. These are not the same as new commercial loans, which pass through the commercial Rand exchange rate (see above), but may include very sizeable investments, as for instance when a Western European super-annuation fund decides to take a stake in the South African bond market;

(b) capital imported by immigrants. If you moved to South Africa, taking the proceeds of the sale of your house and other forms of capital such as life savings with you, then the money would be converted at the financial Rand exchange rate;

(c) the proceeds from the sale of South African securities and equity investments when they are repatriated abroad by non-residents. If you are an American, or Dutch, or any investor who has decided to sell your South African shares, the money that you take out of the country from the proceeds of the sale will be converted to US dollars, or Dutch guilders, at the financial Rand rate of exchange;

Table 5.2   Commercial and Financial Rand Exchange Rates, 1981–89

| | Commercial Rand | | Financial Rand | |
	Effective rate[a]	US$[b,c]	US$[b,d]	Discount on commercial Rand %[e]
	(1)	(2)	(3)	(4)
1981	106.2	1.14	0.80	23.4
1982	92.8	0.92	0.76	18.7
1983	96.8	0.90	–	–
1984	81.1	0.68	–	–
1985	57.3	0.45	0.27	30.2
1986	50.3	0.44	0.22	52.9
1987	52.7	0.49	0.32	38.1
1988	47.3	0.44	0.26	37.9
Jan.	52.4	0.51	0.35	30.6
Feb.	48.9	0.49	0.37	22.7
Mar.	48.5	0.47	0.34	28.6
Apr.	48.5	0.47	0.35	25.1
May	47.3	0.45	0.34	24.5
June	47.1	0.44	0.29	32.5
July	45.9	0.42	0.29	29.6
Aug.	45.3	0.41	0.28	32.2
Sep.	45.3	0.41	0.25	38.7
Oct.	44.5	0.41	0.25	39.1
Nov.	44.9	0.42	0.28	35.2
Dec.	45.8	0.43	0.26	37.9
1989				
Jan.	45.8	0.42	0.26	38.9
Feb.	44.8	0.40	0.25	37.1
Mar.	n.a.	0.39	0.25	37.6
Apr.	n.a.	0.39	0.24	37.8

[a] Weighted average; index 24 January 1979 = 100, figures are average for period.

[b] Units of US currency required to purchase 1 Rand.

[c] Average for period.

[d] End of period rates.

[e] Commercial Rand rate minus financial Rand rate, divided by commercial Rand rate. SARB figures quoted cannot be derived from the two previous columns, because the commercial Rand rate is an average for the period while the financial Rand rate is an end-of-period figure.

n.a. not available.

Source: SARB Quarterly Bulletin, March 1989, p. S80-1, to Feb. 1989; March and April 1989, press reports.

(d) such capital transfers from South Africa to foreign destinations by South African residents as are approved by the authorities. If you are a South African resident and you wish to make a capital payment overseas, say to purchase a company to further develop your business activities, once you have secured approval for the capital transfer involved in the purchase, the financial Rand exchange rate will apply to the purchase of the necessary foreign funds;

(e) capital exports by emigrants. The reverse of (b) above. Emigrant South Africans may take their capital with them only through the financial Rand exchange rate.

How does the financial Rand exchange system work? Rand funds derived from or going to the kinds of transactions outlined above have to be deposited in what are known as 'financial Rand accounts' or 'blocked accounts' which are maintained by the commercial banks. The rate of exchange which applies at any time, and which is quoted by dealers on the Johannesburg stock exchange, is genuinely free floating (that is within its strictly defined limits, this is a clean float). The rate is determined by the balance between the demand for financial Rand (derived from categories (a) and (b) above) and the supply of them (derived from categories (c), (d) and (e) above).

Compared with the commercial Rand, the financial Rand is exchanged at a substantial discount. Figures in US dollar equivalents are given for the period since its reintroduction in 1985 in columns (3) and (4) of Table 5.2.

The degree of discount (the difference between the commercial Rand rate and the financial Rand rate) may be regarded as a crude index of 'disinvestment sentiment', or the *ex ante* excess of supply of financial Rand by those forsaking the South African economy over the demand for financial Rand on the part of new investors and immigrants coming into it. According to this measure, the last quarter of 1986 was the time of maximum pressure from capital outflows, with the financial Rand falling to just under half the value of the commercial Rand. The pressure slackened a little in 1987 and a bit more in 1988, but the fact remains that the substantial discount of the financial Rand (it stood at 38% in March 1989) is evidence of a profound disinclination on the part of the international investing public to become involved in the South African economy.

The real-world effects of these arrangements on the balance of payments are worth explaining in a little detail because they illustrate very well the distorting effects on the economy that are produced by the regime's intransigence about apartheid.

Under the current arrangements, disinvestment by foreign firms, emigration by South African citizens with some financial security, and investment abroad by South African investors, are all discouraged because the exchange rate cost is very high. Intending purchasers of foreign funds for these purposes are being required to pay a premium which is set by the availability of foreign currency coming into South Africa not from all sources, but only from those sources that pass through the financial Rand exchange system. In this sense, capital outflows deriving from disinvestment, emigration and South African investment abroad are 'quarantined', since the Rand sums arising from or for these purposes can only be converted into foreign exchange at the rate which corresponds to a balance between the supply of financial Rands on the one hand and the demand for them from new immigrants and new foreign investments on the other.

To give an example of what this means, American company A decides that it wishes to disinvest from South Africa, and sells its assets to a consortium of its local managers for R10 million. At a commercial Rand exchange rate of US50 cents the proceeds would be worth US$5 million, but the company is not permitted to take its proceeds out in this way. Instead it must pass through the financial Rand exchange system, where the rate may be as low as say 32 cents, yielding only US$3.2 million. Furthermore, a rash of disinvesting companies seeking to repatriate their capital all at once will depress the financial Rand exchange rate still further, raising even higher the cost of pursuing this option.

None of this foreign exchange business puts any pressure on the foreign reserves, however, or on the balance of payments situation, because it is entirely self-limiting. Obviously, as the financial exchange rate drops with the demand for foreign currency to repatriate abroad the funds from disinvestment, there will eventually come a point at which the financial Rand exchange rate has fallen so low as both to discourage any further repatriation of funds and to encourage new investment in South Africa from outside.

To continue the example: if you had recently sold your company in South Africa and did not like the prospect of losing perhaps between a third and a half of your investment through the artificial financial Rand exchange rate, then you could decide to leave your money in South Africa (where, after all, it is still worth R10 million) and use it to purchase local government bonds. The dividends payable on these bonds will be paid to you at the higher commercial Rand exchange rate, which provides yet another incentive to leave your capital in the country.

The importance to South Africa of these arrangements can be seen by reflecting briefly on what the likely consequences would be if, as from February 1983 to August 1985, there were a unified exchange rate. Under these conditions decisions by disinvestors or intending emigrants to take their money out of South Africa would yield more to them in foreign exchange and they would cost the South African economy as a whole a great deal more because they would have a direct impact on the balance of payments. That is, either the country would have to export more and/or import less in order to earn more foreign exchange, or it would be forced to run down the reserves of gold and foreign currency holdings, or it would need to borrow more to cover the deficit on its external account.

Similarly, under a unified exchange rate system, capital inflows from new foreign investors and new migrants would be lower, since there would be no exchange rate incentive for them to want to purchase Rand. Indeed, the balance of payments and external account situation of the economy would probably be so shaky that no sensible investor would want to have anything much to do with it.

These factors make for some substantial difference between the effects on the South African economy of foreign companies' decisions to disinvest, and decisions by foreign bankers to refuse to roll over debt, or to insist on faster repayment of outstanding loans caught inside the 'net'. The loans, when they are eventually repaid, will be paid at the commercial Rand rate, where they will impose a cost on the external account. It was the size of this cost which led to the moratorium in the first place. South Africa did not have the funds and could not afford to meet the cost. The proceeds of disinvestment on the other hand, because they must pass through the financial Rand, impose costs not on the external account but on the domestic South African economy in the form of distortions of domestic savings and investment flows, the degradation of technological and management links, the loss of jobs and labour market diversification, and so on. These issues are all discussed further in chapter six.

We said earlier that the financial Rand was floated in a clean way. Certainly compared to the commercial Rand this is the case. None the less, the South African authorities do have opportunities to intervene in the financial Rand market, and by doing so they can influence the decisions of, for instance, disinvestors who might otherwise leave the South African economy altogether. For example, the SARB has the obligation to approve any proposed royalty or licence arrangement that a foreign disinvestor is making with a local purchaser of the assets. Most disinvestors would probably prefer, under the current rules, to get as much as they can of the value of the assets defined in the contract of sale as royalties or licence fees, since payments defined in this way can then be repatriated abroad through the higher commercial Rand exchange system. Harsh decisions by the SARB not to permit such arrangements have the effect of preventing remittances through the commercial Rand (which is therefore strengthened) and either compelling remittances through the financial Rand (which weakens it, and thus discourages other would-be disinvestors) or forces disinvestors to 'park' their funds in some other investment inside South Africa. This represents a gain for the economy as a whole, not simply in capital terms, but also (as we saw earlier with the 'captive' bank loans) in terms of foreign involvement in the management of funds, and the further development of foreign interest in the actual performance of South African companies and markets.

Conversely, a SARB policy of permitting generous royalty and licence fee payments as part of the sale of capital assets in return for a deal on, let us say, an agreement on the part of the disinvestor to continue to provide intimate technology links with the disinvested firm, would lower the proportion of the funds derived from the asset sale that would be repatriated through the lower financial Rand rate.

Theoretically all of these decisions, involving private sector bargainers and public officials, and on which may hang very considerable sums of money, also provide numerous opportunities for corrupt and fraudulent practices. These are matters that greatly exercise some sections of the South African financial press at the moment, and are another illustration of how the system imposes its own cost on the economy as a whole.

As we saw in Table 5.1, South Africa is suffering a haemorrhage of capital. In the four years from 1985 to 1988 inclusive 25 billion Rand have been recorded in official publications as flowing out of the country. The annual losses in those years were equivalent to 7.7%, 4.4%, 1.9% and 3.5% of GNP respectively. The broad outlines of this flow are set out in Tables 5.3 and 5.4, which show the decline in investments in and loans to South Africa and the increase in South African assets abroad.

A part of the capital flight is accounted for by the repayment of loans in a context in which no new medium- or long-term investment is coming into the country. Since the Leutwiler Accord on rescheduling at the end of March 1986 South Africa

Table 5.3   Foreign Liabilities of South Africa, 1980–86 (R millions)[a](stock of foreign capital in use)

	1980	1981	1982	1983	1984	1985	1986
DIRECT INVESTMENT							
Banking sector	433	776	767	1071	1292	955	845
Long-term	393	443	498	552	554	637	408
Short-term	40	333	269	519	738	318	437
Non-bank private sector	11 880	14 129	16 593	18 248	24 932	26 972	26 706
Long-term	10 230	11 673	12 793	13 598	16 027	17 521	18 096
Short-term	1 650	2 456	3 800	4 650	8 905	9 451	8 610
Total direct investment	12 313	14 905	17 360	19 319	26 224	27 927	27 551
NON-DIRECT INVESTMENT							
Public authorities	1 931	2 393	4 847	5 644	9 171	13 183	11 529
Long-term	1 381	1 871	3 101	3 745	6 544	8 904	8 214
Short-term	550	522	1 746	1 899	2 627	4 279	3 315
Public corporations	4 112	4 484	5 524	6 211	7 672	9 112	9 344
Long-term	4 020	4 420	5 318	6 048	7 462	8 946	9 202
Short-term	92	64	206	163	210	166	142
Banking sector	863	2 987	2 147	3 746	5 787	9 750	5 157
Long-term	242	159	223	717	1 542	379	92
Short-term	621	2 828	1 924	3 029	4 245	9 371	5 065
Non-bank private sector	6 789	8 217	10 727	11 930	19 205	23 489	18 323
Long-term	4 456	5 044	5 563	5 659	7 153	10 232	8 099
Short-term	2 333	3 173	5 164	6 271	12 052	13 257	10 224
Total non-direct investment	13 695	18 081	23 245	27 531	41 835	55 534	44 353
TOTAL FOREIGN LIABILITIES	26 008	32 986	40 605	46 850	68 059	83 461	71 904

[a] The South African authorities have not published any figures for foreign liabilities since the final quarter of 1986.

Source: SARB *Quarterly Bulletin*, March 1989, pp. S72–3.

Table 5.4   Foreign Assets of South Africa, 1980–86 (R millions)[a]

	1980	1981	1982	1983	1984	1985	1986
DIRECT INVESTMENT							
Banking sector	135	81	53	161	102	148	199
Long-term	2	2	2	–	–	–	2
Short-term	133	79	51	161	102	148	197
Non-bank private sector	4 130	5 380	6 767	7 411	12 824	16 485	16 566
Long-term	3 637	4 703	5 886	6 673	11 855	14 880	14 752
Short-term	493	677	881	738	969	1 605	1 814
Total direct investment	4 265	5 461	6 820	7 572	12 926	16 633	16 765
NON-DIRECT INVESTMENT							
Public authorities	999	1 023	1 200	1 521	1 814	2 059	2 591
Long-term	757	739	865	1 205	1 366	1 976	2 463
Short-term	242	284	335	316	448	83	128
Public corporations	268	401	432	421	494	679	791
Long-term	188	217	253	285	296	311	319
Short-term	80	184	179	136	198	368	472
Banking sector	5 930	4 553	4 781	5 231	5 671	6 347	6 000
Long-term	388	505	519	528	561	652	734
Short-term	653	725	836	1 413	1 058	2 050	1 558
Gold reserves	4 854	3 194	3 309	3 250	4 047	3 632	3 708
Special drawing rights	35	129	117	40	5	13	–
Non-bank private sector	1 884	2 020	2 152	2 424	3 711	4 543	5 967
Long-term	494	616	674	812	1 432	1 477	1 642
Short-term	1 390	1 404	1 478	1 612	2 279	3 066	4 325
Total non-direct investment	9 081	7 997	8 565	9 597	11 690	13 628	15 349
TOTAL FOREIGN ASSETS	13 346	13 458	15 385	17 169	24 616	30 261	32 114

[a] The South African authorities have not published any figures for foreign assets since the final quarter of 1986.

Source: SARB *Quarterly Bulletin*, March 1989, pp. S74–5.

has repaid more than R10 billion of foreign debt, though the great bulk of this, approximately 80% (including its 1982 loan from the IMF) lay outside the 'net'. Under the Stals Accord of twelve months later, South Africa is committed to paying approximately US$150 million of principal on debt caught inside the 'net' every six months through to the end of June 1990, when the agreement expires. As we saw in chapter four, the Stals Accord contains clauses offering creditors the option of a ten-year arrangement for complete repayment, or of converting the debt into South African equities within the financial Rand exchange rate system. There has been little enthusiasm for the equities option, but some banks have already agreed to the ten-year proposal, and our information suggests (as we said in chapter four) that some others may decide to follow suit before June 1990.

These developments are not going to solve the problem of capital flight from South Africa, however, because debt repayment in the absence of new loans is only a part of the equation. The other part is the departure of domestic South African capital. Only a relatively small part of this can be accounted for by disinvestment on the part of foreign firms, and we look at this aspect in chapter six. Most of it has to be explained by the rapid expansion of South African investment overseas. In this context the recent worldwide publicity that attached to the attempt by Minorco, part of the Oppenheimer empire of companies, to take over Consolidated Gold Fields (though the takeover failed in mid-May 1989) has had a symbolic quality to it. South African capital is looking for investment opportunities outside South Africa where political risks will be lower, the difficulties of sanctions less onerous, and the prospects for profits – given the increasingly high costs of regulation and coercion in the South African economy – rather higher.

When a South African resident wishes to transfer capital out of South Africa approval has to be obtained from the SARB. Many transfers thought quite normal in other countries are simply not permitted. For instance, transfers for the purpose of purchasing shares on a foreign stock exchange are not allowed, though minor exceptions may be approved from time to time, for instance for the purchase of rights arising from existing share holdings or to enable arbitrage operations by South African brokers. In terms of quantity, however, these permits are trivial. The basic rule is that investment in equities abroad is simply not permitted because of the loss of foreign exchange that it would involve.

When companies wish to invest abroad the SARB has a policy of examining each case on its merits. The merits are usually seen as being ones of long-term development of trade opportunities, or the protection of what are thought of as strategic market links – generally, investments that will permit the avoidance of sanctions, say by creating new brass plate companies in non-inquisitive states through which trading operations can, at least on paper, be directed. (It is worth noting, *inter alia*, that the South African Board of Trade and Industries has numerous export incentive schemes for South African companies seeking foreign markets. These can include 100% reimbursement for the costs of investigating possible new markets, including travel and accommodation costs!) Under the published rules for investing in foreign assets, all outgoing investment of this kind ought to occur through the financial Rand exchange rate, but the SARB has apparently been known to permit at least a portion of such funds to be remitted at the higher commercial Rand rate for what it regards as worthwhile cases. In these instances it will not normally permit the whole sum to pass through the commercial Rand exchange rate, presumably on the grounds that if South Africa had a unitary exchange rate its level would probably lie somewhere between the commercial and financial Rand.

The complexity of the arrangements, and presumably also their occasional quality of serendipity, coupled with the anxiety of many white South Africans to protect their security in the event of a further serious deterioration in political stability, seems to have led to considerable illegal exporting of capital.

In the nature of things these developments are hard to prove and impossible to quantify. Some South African bankers reported to us, however, that they were conscious of a systematic apparent decline in the profitability of small- and medium-sized companies among their clients, and that they suspected that these declines were related to foreign invoicing procedures. To give an example, a small widget manufacturer, who until now has imported widget components from a West German supplier, decides instead to set up a subsidiary in Switzerland to purchase and export the components to South Africa direct. In doing so the subsidiary, in small but regular amounts, increases the invoiced price of the components. The head office, in paying the augmented price which it is entitled to do through the commercial Rand exchange rate, is effectively exporting its own profits and hence its capital. Tax departments in other developed economies have long been familiar with invoice related tax-avoidance procedures, many of which were invented by international corporations some of which have their origins in South Africa (Pallister et al. 1988, 130–45). Now South Africa appears to be experiencing similar developments with, as their objective, the beating of the exchange control regulations.

In response to this and other developments the regime has taken a number of administrative steps (*Financial Mail* 10 February 1989, p. 41). In July 1988 the Banks Act was amended to extend the right of the SARB to inspect the business activities of individuals or companies which, though not registered as banking institutions, were suspected of taking deposits from the public.

In the second week of December 1988 a working group was set up at the request of the Minister of Finance to examine various completed foreign exchange transactions in response to information that had come to light suggesting new methods of avoidance.

The Governor of the SARB, Gerhard de Kock, announced at the beginning of February 1989 that the bank was taking a number of measures to improve exchange control methods of enforcement. A Senior Deputy-Governor of the bank was to assume the specific responsibility of co-ordinating the exchange control and banking supervision departments of the bank, and both departments were to be expanded, with new inspectors recruited. Simultaneously the exchange control department was to take outside advice from accountants and other government departments in the search for methods for detecting and preventing over-invoicing of imports, and other fraudulent methods of avoiding exchange control of capital exports.

These developments are suggestive. One criticism of the current state of social and political decay in contemporary South Africa that comes not simply out of their own anti-apartheid movement, but also from the financial and political press, is that there is widespread corruption and fraud, and a fear that the increasing layers of administrative regulation, coupled with the nervousness generated by the country's political uncertainties, are adding to this climate of moral decline. Our impression from the sketchy evidence at our disposal in the one area of international financial links is that this fear may not be misplaced.

Whether it leads to corrupt practices or not, the administrative regulation of exchange controls at the intensity now practised by the South African authorities, certainly leads both to rapidly rising enforcement costs and to inefficiency. In theory the freedom for investors to put their capital wherever in the world they expect they can achieve the best return ('best' being dependent on whether they seek the highest, the most secure, or whatever) would be to South Africa's advantage. However a concern simply to prevent capital flight, and to try to ensure that it is put to use in the domestic economy, means that the authorities are not in a position to permit the free capital markets that are a notable feature of the rest of the modern developed world. The result is that South African investments are not being allocated efficiently, in the sense of being put to work where investors expect high and/or secure returns, but are being channelled either wholly into the domestic economy or into sanctions – breaking arrangements or (often by illegal means) into safe havens from apartheid.

One effect of this is that although South Africa records gross holdings by residents of some R17 billion of direct investment in foreign non-financial assets (Table 5.4, 1986, total direct investment), only a very small amount of this could actually be mobilised by the regime in the event of another serious financial crisis. Many of these assets are encumbered by debt (borrowing abroad by South African entities registered in foreign countries is not illegal, to our knowledge, in any of the countries currently applying restrictions on loans to South Africa), so that their net value is less than their gross value. And in any event, many of these foreign holdings, however they were acquired, represent, in the current climate of domestic uncertainty bordering on fear, a form of insurance against exactly the type of economic collapse in which the authorities might seek to have them repatriated. A reasonable expectation would surely be that the sort of circumstances in which the authorities did attempt such a thing would be ones in which they would be least likely to secure compliance.

Against the trend, it is worth mentioning that there have been some capital inflows to South Africa over the past five years, but official sources do not clearly identify their origins. The amounts are not large, and almost certainly consist mainly of trade credits of a short-term variety. (We have more to say about trade credits in chapter six.) There is some fragmentary evidence to suggest that longer-term investment may have been provided by at least one Far Eastern financial centre, but we have not been able to identify the source or quantify the amount. Chapter six contains details on the particular situation in each possible investing country with respect to new investment in South Africa.

Private portfolio investors continue to show an interest in South African investments, but even when there is a surge in such activity, as in the fourth quarter of 1987 and the third quarter of 1988, when R73 million and R75 million respectively of new funds went into the stock and bond markets from private foreign investors through the financial Rand exchange system, the funds were of comparatively small amounts.

These sorts of investments increasingly take on the appearance of classic high risk/high return propositions, since the uncertainties of the South African investment environment may be off-set by movements in the exchange rates. For example, municipal paper traded on the Johannesburg stock exchange in early 1988 was yielding 17% interest. Since investment in this sector is via the financial Rand (at a discount) and interest is payable through the commercial Rand, the actual rate of return to a foreign investor would have been of the order of 25% per annum. South African securities purchased by foreigners can be sold abroad, but investors run the risk of further, and possibly sharp, devaluations. An additional consideration to take into account is that, assuming a period of relative stability in South African markets (which is a large and in our view unwarranted assumption), then the possibility of trading and profit-taking in South African securities between both South African and foreign stock exchanges will have the effect, over time, of inflating their Rand price on the Johannesburg exchange and deflating their foreign currency price on international exchanges until the yields in the different markets converge. At that point, the incentive to put money into South Africa, even on the part of the keen and sharp-eyed investor, will evaporate altogether. The sums that are actually involved at present in private portfolio investment in South Africa, however, are trivial in comparison with its needs. Why it cannot secure access to the world's stocks of savings that are so essential to it is the opening theme of chapter six.

CHAPTER SIX

South Africa's Problem with Capital Flows

South Africa needs foreign capital to replenish the capital stock of the economy as a whole (which as we saw in chapters three and five is diminishing); to meet its international debt obligations, which in 1990 will be onerous; and to further develop its economy, which, as we saw in chapter three is now, and will be increasingly, in need of substantial investment to help in the resolution of pressing social and political problems. We have seen in the preceding chapters that foreign capital is not being imported into South Africa and domestic capital, over the past four years, has been draining away in great quantities. In this chapter we examine the international reasons for this, and review the capital situation with respect to medium- and long-term credits; short-term credits, mainly for trade purposes; and the processes of investment and disinvestment, through which many foreign companies are leaving South Africa.

Medium- and Long-term Credits

Reliable data on the sources of financial flows into South Africa are not available, but the qualitative material that we present here has been systematically assembled with the assistance of numerous sources in the international banking arena, and its reliability tested wherever possible.

One reason why so few foreign financial institutions are making medium- and long-term loans available to South African entities is that the governments of the Western world have either made it illegal for them to do so, or have adopted a policy of official discouragement (UN 1989a and b). In the United States the Comprehensive Anti-Apartheid Legislation of November 1986 prohibits all loans to the South African government or its agencies (this affects mainly the banking sector in the US) and also prohibits all loans by American citizens, no matter where they reside, to South African borrowers. There are a few exceptions to do with educational, welfare and humanitarian objectives, and it is generally agreed that trade credits are also excluded from the prohibition. As we pointed out earlier, however, some banks had already responded to state and city pressure to stop lending to the South African government and its agencies as early as 1977, and the deteriorating situation in South Africa during 1984 and 1985 led to an intensification of these pressures. It was publicity attaching to the decision by Chase Manhattan Bank not to roll over maturing short-term credits, and to close unused credit lines, that is widely believed to have sparked the 1985 foreign exchange crisis.

All United States banks are very conscious of the important role played in their immediate commercial environment by the pressures of public opinion, the more so when these pressures are exerted by important and/or wealthy clients such as large city administrations or prominent university institutions. Many of them are also profoundly pessimistic about the future of South African society, which acts as a disincentive for continued participation. One bank said that South African social policies generated too many constraints on their business to make ownership or management of a banking business in South Africa worth while; that they were unable to provide a secure environment there for their professional staff (which was a high priority for the bank) and that they could not get free of the net of anti-apartheid legislation in the US, which was getting tighter. The attraction of the 1997 option for those

American banks with loans trapped in the 'net' seemed to be that it offered the cleanest way of severing their links permanently. It seems clear to us that US capital is now completely off limits to South Africa, and that South African entities, whether public or private, have no real prospects of getting back to it in the foreseeable future.

The countries of the Commonwealth agreed at their Heads of Government meeting in Nassau in 1985 to ban all new government loans to the government of South Africa, and later adopted voluntary bans on new lending by commercial banks to South African entities. In Britain voluntary restraint needed little encouragement. Banks there are very unenthusiastic about further lending to South Africa, some like Barclays having already announced a decision to provide no further loans, and all are sceptical of the future stability of the South African investment environment. Most also have acute concerns about their corporate images and the prospects for other business if they continue lending to South Africa, and so may tend to be deterred by the high visibility of South African lending. The temptation to put their loans currently caught inside the 'net' into the ten-year option results from an analysis that suggests that South Africa is unlikely to be able to sustain the long sequence of large current account surpluses that will be necessary to service and repay all the outstanding loans, and that sooner or later some creditors will miss payments. They believe that priority will be accorded to those who took the longer-term option. Their efforts are directed at trying to secure the return of moneys already lent. They are not in a position to contemplate further lending while previous lending remains outstanding well beyond its due date for repayment. Leaving their money in until 1997 may, some of them hope, absolve them from having to devote further decision-making time to the question of new loans. To add further discouragement, the Bank of England matrix requirements for provisioning of sovereign debt to South Africa call for provisions (that is capital set aside as security against defaults) in the 5 to 15% band. This is a further disincentive to undertake new lending, because provisioning at this level significantly reduces profit margins. It is, however, a significantly less stringent provision than the Bank of England imposes on lending to problem debtors in Latin America, which ranges up to 30% or 40%.

Elsewhere in the Commonwealth, Canada imposed a ban on lending to the South African government in 1985, and followed this up a year later with a voluntary ban on new bank lending to South African entities. Canadian authorities are sure the embargo is being complied with, and Canadian banks' exposure in South Africa has gone down by $50 million since it was imposed. The Canadian government was embarrassed early in 1989 by publicity surrounding the fact that the Bank of Nova Scotia was involved in making credit available to Minorco (the international company controlled by Anglo-American, the South African multinational) in its bid to take over Consolidated Gold Fields. Some anti-apartheid opinion might take the view that these loans were improper. Whether they were or were not in breach of the principle of the Canadian embargo, the issue involves a number of reasonably complex arguments to which we return in chapter eight. We note at this point, however, that since the loans lay outside the Rand monetary area, and were for the purchase of assets located abroad, these loans could not possibly have been making any contribution to South Africa's balance of payments situation. As with the situation with Swiss banks (see below), the Minorco bid is further evidence of the flight of capital out of South Africa, rather than a manoeuvre to shore up South Africa's eroding capital base.

The Australians requested a voluntary ban from their financial institutions on all forms of lending to South Africa in 1985, and, although they cannot be 100% certain, the Australian authorities are confident that the ban is being complied with. The Malaysian government has had legislation in force since shortly after independence, prohibiting contact with South Africa. The Malays say that the legislation is strictly administered: it prohibits all loans, and even bans visits to Malaysia by South African business people, bankers, and government representatives. The government of Singapore has imposed a ban on all imports from South Africa and it is official policy to discourage banks from extending finance to South Africa. No indigenous Singaporean banks had loans caught in the 1985 moratorium and none had any loans to South African nationals outstanding as at 31 January 1988. The authorities advise that Singaporean banks have not provided finance to local firms to support their exports to South Africa. While banks in Singapore have received visits from South African representatives, such visits have been few and were in the nature of courtesy calls. South Africans have made approaches seeking credits but have been refused.

The EEC Council of Ministers decided at its meeting in 1986 to ban new loans to South Africa of a duration longer than five years, leaving the implementation of this policy up to each member country. In France a licensing system is employed. Any firm that wants to transfer funds to South Africa requires authorisation from the Ministry of Finance, and this authority under the current policy is refused for anything other than short-term trade credits (under eighteen months). French banks, with FF 14 billion caught in the 'net', are the third largest creditors, with 14% of South Africa's international credit exposure, after the United Kingdom (25%) and the United States (just under 20%). FF 6 billion of this total is accounted for by loans associated with the building of South Africa's nuclear power station (a French project), so the debt is more highly concentrated than that of other countries. French banks do not appear to be attracted by either of the two conversion options offered by the South African authorities, but their view of the ten-year option may have been changing recently in the light of the American (Brady) proposals on the debt problem of Less Developed Countries (LDCs). The French government (which made proposals in 1988 for an international initiative sharply to reduce LDC debt levels) appears to favour this new American approach, which envisages rescheduling periods of from seven to fifteen years, with periods of grace (during which

payments would be suspended, as with the South African
proposal, which offers no repayments for the two years after
1990) of up to five years duration. Government officials stress,
however, that South Africa is a special case, requiring separate
treatment.

What is clear is that French banks currently do not experience any of the shareholder, client or public pressure critical
of their links with South Africa which banks in Britain, the US
and West Germany experience. One French bank reported that
it did not believe it had ever received a single letter about its
attitude towards South Africa, and that the subject of apartheid
had never once been discussed at either board or annual
meetings. This situation may be changing, however. Government officials detect a much greater awareness of South Africa
on the part of the French public, particularly among young
people, and politicians are now conscious of the extent to
which media coverage of the issue has increased and deepened. Government concern also flows from the view that
South Africa might come to have a higher political profile in
the black African countries with which France has particularly
close relations (mainly the former colonial, French-speaking
territories of west, Saharan, and north Africa), and that the
volume and importance of French banking interests in those
countries should lead to a greater prudence on the part of
French banks in their dealings with South Africa itself.

In West Germany the banking supervisors require all German banks to make provisions for outstanding loans to South
Africa, and the effect of this is that no German bank is lending
to South Africa for longer than twelve months. Senior banking
officials are generally well disposed towards South Africa, but
have been profoundly influenced by the pressure exerted by
the anti-apartheid movement, especially through the protest-
ant churches. One bank reported that it had perhaps 1% of its
investments in South Africa, but had to devote 60% of its time
to the issue, saying that as a result they felt 'battle worn' and
had 'given up'. They were also conscious of the importance
that the issue had now assumed for the West German

government, and believed that as a result normal banking arrangements between themselves and South African clients could not be resumed until apartheid had been dismantled. They were also fairly clear about what they thought this meant in practice, a subject to which we return in chapter eight.

Italian banks were fairly heavily involved in South Africa in the 1960s and 1970s, when a number of major engineering projects involved Italian contractors, but their presence there has declined since. A number of Italian banks have loans caught in the moratorium, but not sufficient to make them members of the Technical Committee. They seem to be fatalistic about the future of this money, and have not yet taken a position on the 1997 option. They have no expectation that South Africa will be in a position to repay in 1990, and are pessimistic about the short- and medium-term prospects for the South African economy. They report a lot of active interest in Italian banking business by visiting South African executives, but the Italian government prohibits all medium- and long-term lending to South Africa, and no one expects this situation to change in the immediate future.

The three largest Belgian banks all had sufficiently large funds trapped in the 1985 moratorium to be included in the group of thirty that originally met Dr Leutwiler. They were not subsequently members of the smaller Technical Committee, however. None of them has announced an interest in the 1997 option, though one Belgian bank has exercised the option of repatriating a proportion of its exposure via the South African equities market and the financial Rand exchange rate. All Belgian banks are circumspect about further business with South Africa, and have made provisions against their current exposure. The 1997 option does not appeal to them mainly because they doubt the ability of the South African economy, so long as it is excluded from world capital markets, to generate sufficient foreign exchange to sustain the schedule of repayments.

Dutch commercial banks agreed to stop lending to the South African government or its agencies in 1976, but they did continue to make small credits available to the South African private sector, and some small loans of this kind were caught in the 'net' in 1985. Dutch banks are required to report all South African dealings to the central bank, and no medium- or long-term loans are being made available to any South African borrowers.

In Western Europe outside of the EEC, restrictions on loans to South Africa are, if anything, even more strict.

The Nordic countries agreed on a common 'Program of Action Against Apartheid' in 1985. This program prohibits almost all trade with South Africa, and since it was agreed Denmark, Norway, Finland, Iceland and Sweden have all passed legislation making loans to South African entities illegal.

In Austria the banking system is largely in public ownership (both central and municipal governments own banks) and so is subject to shareholder pressure of rather a different kind from that of other Western countries. Unlike the Nordic states, Austria appears to have had a few loans caught in the 1985 moratorium, and some of these may have consisted of debt purchased in the early 1980s from US banks deciding to quit South Africa in response to client pressures. The Austrians prefer to maintain a general reserve against loan losses, rather than operate (as all other European banks do) country-specific provisions. However, their exposure to South Africa has never been large, and appears to have declined in the past few years, suggesting that they may have sold debt, or exercised the equity conversion option. It is this that lends some credence to the reports that they may have purchased US debt a few years ago: they can afford to sell cheaply now because they bought cheaply in the first place.

The Swiss banks are an enigma. The secrecy of their banking system is a part of its success, and jealously guarded. The Swiss authorities have expressed their opposition to economic sanctions against South Africa, but are also committed to not allowing their country to become a route through which sanctions can be avoided. As we saw earlier (Table 4.1) they have imposed a ceiling, or cap, on medium- and long-term lending (longer than twelve months) to South Africa, and this cap has not been exceeded. Swiss banks must report all South African loan activities to the authorities, and in the past four years lending has been very small indeed. None the less, we have been struck by the numbers of our interlocutors outside Switzerland who remain convinced that Swiss banks are currently a source of credit for South Africa. We have, however, despite repeated requests for it, been given no evidence for this view, and since there is no published evidence to show that, apart from trade credits, South Africa is in receipt of substantial loans from any source, it is perhaps difficult to see why these rumours persist. One reason might be gold swaps. This is an exchange of gold for credit at an agreed rate of interest over an agreed period of time. Swiss banks have done this kind of business with South Africa in the past. It is not possible to secure evidence on whether they are doing any of it at the moment.

What can be said is that the major South African multinational companies operate numerous subsidiaries in Switzerland, and have major banking connections there; that a great proportion of the South African gold trade passes through the refineries that are located in Switzerland; that since the Central Selling Organisation of de Beers moved the world diamond market from London to Switzerland the quantity of banking services provided and consumed by the corporation and its clients must have risen sharply; that there is a history of close contacts between Swiss banks and wealthy South African companies and individuals; and that the unique character of the banking arrangements provided in Switzerland, including the secrecy, may be an obstacle to persuading world opinion of their true role. It is betraying no confidences, nor we imagine creating any surprises, to say that alone of all the banking operations of the Western world, none of the major Swiss commercial banks agreed to talk to us.

None of this is evidence to suggest that the Swiss are giving comfort to South Africa by providing badly needed foreign loans. On the contrary, what it does suggest is that Switzerland, increasingly, may be an important conduit and/or haven for South African capital that is fleeing the country. This may be providing some sort of comfort to some South Africans, but these can hardly be said to include the regime, which would much rather that it stopped. We refer to this theme again in chapter eight.

The Japanese imposed a voluntary ban on bank loans to South Africa in 1974 and repeated this request to their commercial banks in 1987. Japanese financial institutions are complying voluntarily with this request, which in any event is endorsed by their own perception of the effects of non-compliance on their business opportunities in the United States. Increasingly US cities, states, corporations, educational institutions and trusts are adopting the practice of screening banks for their South African connections before agreeing to do business with them. The one area of uncertainty in the field of financial links between South Africa and Japan would be the giant Japanese corporations, which act as their own bankers and generate substantial capital flows within their own operations without recourse to outside finance. In the absence of evidence to the contrary, the judgement must be that although these corporations might be extending normal short-term credits associated with export sales to South Africa, they are not providing extended credit or loans to South Africa. Certainly in the financial year 1988–89, in response to their own government's requests, Japanese traders reduced their imports from South Africa (down 3.5% in the first half of the year). Not lending would also be consistent with post-war Japanese industrial and trade policy of generally avoiding giving offence to the more powerful interests, and concentrating on market success in areas of growth and strategic economic importance. Though some South African mineral resources are important to Japan, though Japan is South Africa's most important trading partner in Asia, and though South Africa has been keen to diversify its trade to the Far East, and thus Japan in particular over recent years (not least because of North American and European hostility), the reality is that South Africa is not important enough in world trade to count much in Japan.

The Hong Kong financial world, in keeping with the rather unusual constitutional status of the Crown Colony, has experienced no public or political pressures over South Africa, and approaches the question of credits entirely on the assessment of risk. Since the moratorium, in which a number of Hong Kong banks had loans trapped, further credits to South Africa have been refused. In 1988 they were believed still to be considering their attitude towards the 1997 option included in the Stals Accord. This also seems to have been the position of banks in Taiwan, who emphasise strong concern at the risks involved in lending to South Africa at the moment. None the less, a delegation of Taiwanese bankers is reported (Hirsch 1989 (forthcoming), 27) to have visited South Africa in October 1988, and controls over the export of capital from Taiwan have recently been relaxed. The important element in the assessment of risks by the Taiwanese is likely to be the United States, whose market is of dominant importance for them and to whose preferences they are sensitive. On trade finance, however, they are doubtless able to go their own way rather more, and in the context of their rapidly expanding trade with South Africa it is reasonable to assume that their banks are doing plenty of trade credit business. The situation is evolving in much the same way in the Republic of Korea, which until recently was a capital-importing country, and not a capital exporter. We discuss the importance of these countries in the provision of trade finance below.

The Thai government prohibits trade, including financial links, with South Africa, and we can find no evidence of loans or credits being made available to South Africa by either the Arab petroleum exporting countries or Israel, which in September 1987 banned all new investment in and government loans to South Africa.

A brisk and necessarily qualitative survey of this kind can give only an impression, though we think reasonably systematic, of the current situation. We can illustrate what that situation costs in practical business terms in South Africa, by reference to the recent announcement (*Financial Mail*, 10 February 1989, 79–80) of the 1989 borrowing requirement of South Africa's electricity supply corporation (Eskom).

Eskom needs to borrow R3.81 billion in 1989, an increase of 61% over its financing requirements in the previous year. It proposes to raise this money in the following variety of markets (1988 figures in brackets):

Local South African bond market: R1.5 billion (R683 m);
Local South African money market: R981 million (R244 m);
Swap cash flows: R1.12 billion (R504 m);
Export credit finance: R211 million (R388 m);
Foreign loans: nil (R552 m from the PIC, that is loans from the funds caught in the 'net', which were thus not new loans to South Africa, though the money was new to Eskom).

Corporate demand for funds of this kind is putting great pressure on the domestic South African financial market, which presumably explains Eskom's rather greater reliance in 1989 compared with 1988 on a bond market issue, which no doubt will be pushed hard abroad. The truth, however, is that Eskom (and the many other borrowers who would like to have credit from the domestic capital market but won't be able to because of Eskom's being there ahead of them) would much prefer to borrow abroad if it could. Eskom financial managers continue to meet European bankers with this objective in mind, but one of them is quoted as saying: 'Politically, it's just not possible for us to raise new [foreign] loans. But we're heartened by recent Swiss rollovers. The situation is more positive than even six months ago'.

These expressions of optimism do not much accord with our findings. For instance, one reason why new foreign issues of South African bonds might not attract a good reception internationally is that outstanding bonds are trading at a substantial discount on the secondary market.

Trade Credits

Trade credit and the financing of trade flows generally is a field of some technical complexity. Here we offer only a brief survey, with some introductory background material.

A trade credit is an advance of money to enable sellers and purchasers to make and close international deals across great distances and (sometimes) times. A credit may be made available for anything from thirty days to ten years, depending on the commodity that is being traded. The long-term trade credit periods generally relate to major engineering or construction projects, or capital goods (such as jet airliners) in which the supply of custom-built equipment may involve long leads and lags (George & Giddy 1983). Generally international trade in primary and manufactured goods in financed with letters of credit of 30- to 180-day duration, while credits for industrial and agricultural equipment may run from 180 days to five years.

Most trade credit is arranged either by the supplier or the buyer, and these are referred to as supplier credits and buyer credits. Banks participate in this activity by lending the money for the credits, but they are not the only agencies to do so. Generally when banks are involved they will provide the credit from beginning to end of a transaction, but occasionally they may enter during the period of a credit, purchasing from a supplier the paper (credit document) at a discount in what is called an *a forfait* transaction.

Most banking business from the United Kingdom and the United States which involves South Africa is done through correspondent banking facilities. Barclays, the Midland Bank and Standard Chartered, from Britain, and Citicorp, Chase Manhattan, and Manufacturers Hanover Trust from the US, have sold (disinvested) their South African banking operations. However, seven German banks, four French banks, and three major Swiss banks currently operate branches or representative offices in South Africa and therefore continue to have strong commercial links with the country. All of them are in a position to provide both buyer and supplier credits in each direction. The Japanese now have regulations prohibiting their financial institutions from maintaining a physical presence in South Africa, and the Bank of Tokyo closed its South African office in 1986.

Since the Second World War the governments of most countries have sought to promote trade through official export credit agencies. These are usually government or government sponsored agencies which offer insurance against loss for finance houses undertaking trade credit finance, and/or actual loans. Government export credit agencies talk of having countries 'on cover' or 'off cover' for the insurance of short-, medium- and long-term trade credit finance. If a country is 'on cover' then a bank that has been approached by one of its clients to provide it with credit to fill an overseas order (broadly, to package, transport and deliver) can cover itself against loss by taking out insurance with the export credit agency. The bank then provides the credit to the supplier, passing on the insurance premium as part of the cost, and charging interest for the loan. If the deal falters in some way (a ship lost at sea; material damage on arrival; bankrupcy of the ordering party), then the export credit agency, under the insurance policy, refunds the credit to the bank. Having a country 'on cover' is therefore the critical issue. Without it Western banks are reluctant to lend for trade purposes because of the risks. With it, they are only too delighted to do so because it is effectively risk free.

In general the share of world trade that is financed through export credit agencies has been falling in recent years. The agencies were very badly hit by the world debt crisis, and many of them are now under a certain amount of pressure from their own governments. A view has emerged in recent years that the agencies may have been working as export subsidy tools in disguise, a role that would be discouraged by, for instance, the OECD committees on export credit policy.

The availability of trade credits is not going to ease a country's balance of payments problems except in the sense that they may help it to trade its way, medium and long term, out of imbalance on its visible account. They cannot ease its capital flow situation, however, since they exist only to facilitate trade, and cannot be employed to settle other sorts of debt.

International statistics for short-term trade credits (the 30 to 180 days variety) are notoriously poor because they are very difficult to collect. According to one estimate, South Africa's short-term debt, composed of trade credits guaranteed by official agencies, fell from US$8.4 billion at the end of 1986 to US$7.56 billion a year later. Another estimate suggests that South Africa's outstanding trade credits stood at $6.9 billion at the end of 1986 (Lind & Koistinen 1988, 17).

However the figure is arrived at, in world trade credit terms it is small. Its smallness reflects the fact that South Africa is a relatively insignificant participant in international trade, with (outside of Africa) a relatively small economy.

Ninety per cent of the officially insured trade credit comes from the countries that are South Africa's major trading partners (the United Kingdom, West Germany, France) where South Africa is still 'on cover', but the official agencies and the banks all say that there is very little demand for business. The Exim Bank of the United States offers only restricted cover on credits for South African trade, and several smaller American agencies have South Africa 'off cover' altogether. None of the American banks to whom we talked was providing short-term trade credits, and one major US bank reported that it was not making any loans available to any American company engaged in trading or other transactions with South Africa.

In France there is evidence to suggest that banks would be prepared to provide large, longer-term trade finance for South Africa if the business existed, but only if they could pass the cover over to COFACE (the French export credit insurance agency). Current government policy would probably prevent this from happening.

The Germans have four separate export agencies, two of which provide guarantees only, in the manner of the UK

Export Credit Guarantee Department. These are the Hermes Kreditversicherungs, and the Treuarbeit. In addition, the Kreditanstalt fuer Wiederaufbau (public), and the AKA-Ausfuhrkredit (private: a consortium of banking interests), both provide export credits. Bankers in West Germany say they are continuing to provide short-term credits for South African trade, but only where they support German exports. Together, France and West Germany recorded the lion's share of the 24% growth in OECD imports from South Africa in the first half of 1988, but how much of this trade was financed by credits made available in those countries we are not able to say. German bankers claimed that there was very little trade credit business to be had either to or from South Africa.

The Swiss have no limit on short-term trade finance by their banks, but they do monitor the flows, and report that there has been no sudden increase in the provision of trade credits, and no evidence to suggest that Swiss finance houses are now providing the finance for trade which would have been financed elsewhere if it were not for sanctions.

The Dutch government export credit insurance agency (NCIA) has South Africa 'off cover' for all exposures, and the Belgian equivalent (OND), though in principle it is open for cover for all maturities, in practice applies a limit on total commitments and (as part of the trade sanctions policy of the EC) carefully scrutinises individual transactions. The Italian agency (SACE) raised its maturity limit on export credits from twelve to twenty-four months in 1987, but it won't cover exposures for longer than this, and still rates South Africa three out of three, which is the lowest of its credit ratings. The Austrian credit insurance agency (OeKB) has South Africa 'off cover' for trade credits of longer than twelve months duration. Very little business is being written with South Africa in any of these countries.

The Far East probably now contributes the great bulk of those trade credits that are not made available by Britain, the Federal Republic of Germany and France. The Japanese have South Africa 'on cover' by both of their export credit agencies, the Export Import bank (EID) which provides both credits and guarantees, and the Ministry of International Trade and Industry (MITI), which provides only guarantees. Both consider applications for trade credit finance on the merits of each case put up to them. The volume of insured credits outstanding in Japan is substantial, and is augmented by the practice of some Japanese institutions of providing finance for trade to Japanese shippers, with bills due on the date the South African buyer is scheduled to settle. This arrangement facilitates Japanese exports, but does not involve support for any South African entities. Japanese banks may be providing finance to South African importers by making working capital available to Japanese companies selling in that market, thus enabling those companies to extend credit to their local South African importers. We cannot estimate the volume of these transactions.

Perhaps of even greater interest is the role now being played by Hong Kong and Taiwanese banks in the supply of trade credits for South African business.

We have received reports, which we cannot confirm, that a considerable volume of trade to and from South Africa is currently documented in and financed from Hong Kong, without ever actually passing through the colony itself.

Taiwanese banks may be creating similar business opportunities. Taiwan is South Africa's second largest Asian trading partner after Japan, and a rapidly growing market which South Africa is actively pursuing. The Republic has opened a permanent showroom at the Taipei World Trade Centre, and it is widely assumed that Taiwan's imports of gold from South Africa will be rising sharply since the lifting in 1987 of Taiwan's former restrictions on private trading in gold. Increasing trade flows will presumably be being financed by Taiwanese banks. Similar developments seem likely to be in train in the Republic of Korea, where, although trade with South Africa is not large, it is growing, and the local banks will be providing the financial credits for it. It seems entirely likely that South Africa will identify South Korea as a future significant trading partner and start to put resources into developing the relationship as it has done with Taiwan.

Of all the rapidly expanding economies of the North Asian region, Thailand is the one that seems closed to South Africa. Its government has imposed an official ban on South African trade and has been known to confiscate goods that come from there. Nevertheless there is a substantial diamond trade in Thailand and this must surely include South African stones, but since the industry pays cash for the gems no trade finance is involved.

Export credit agencies in Australia, Canada, New Zealand and the Nordic countries all have South Africa 'off cover'. The voluntary ban on lending to South Africa by Australian financial institutions extends to include short-term trade credits, as well as all other lending.

Investment and Disinvestment

In terms of the rest of the world, the South African economy is relatively small, smaller than the economies of either Argentina or Austria for instance. As we have seen, however, in terms of the economies of southern Africa it is large and dominant, with complex inter-relations both internally and across its borders into the rest of Africa, and with a developed infrastructure of transport and communications. It is important to emphasise that although South Africa is being starved of capital the effects of this are not uniform, or simple either to observe or to understand. The economy is still capable of levels of growth up to 2% per annum, so that investment is still taking place. The sources of this investment have, however, clearly changed in the past ten years. We can see this by looking at the pattern of capital accumulation in South Africa on the part of foreign countries. For instance, in 1966 United States companies' direct investments in South Africa totalled US$490 million. By 1981 total assets had expanded to US$2.6 billion, but according to US Commerce Department statistics this total had declined by the end of 1987 to US$1.6 billion (Cooper 1989,

9). Some of this decline in asset value is due to the devaluation of the Rand. Some is due to disinvestment by American companies in response to the pressures from the anti-apartheid campaign in the US. Some is surely due to disinvestment in response to declining profitability in a deteriorating economy.

The pattern of investment from foreign sources is further clouded by the difference in regulations applied by foreign states. For instance Japan does not permit direct investment in South Africa by Japanese companies, but Japan is an increasingly important trading partner with South Africa and a number of Japanese companies maintain a presence there either through companies that are registered outside Japan (e.g. Ajinomoto Co. Inc. which maintains a business in Johannesburg through its Brazilian subsidiary Ajinomoto Interamericana Industria E. Comercio Ltd) or through licensing, distribution, trademark, technological or franchising agreements (e.g. Fanuc Ltd of Tokyo, whose South African agent, named Fanuc Ltd, is licensed to use the name and to service Fanuc products throughout the Republic) (Cooper 1988, 189–202). Furthermore, the chains of investment, company to company, are often long and complex, posing problems of both measurement and analysis. For instance, Gulf and Western Inc., the US entertainments conglomerate, through one of its subsidiaries owns 100% of the equity in Gulf and Western B.V. of the Netherlands, which in turn owns 33% of the equity in United International Pictures B.V., which owns 95% of the equity in UIP S.A., a South African company which distributes films. Gulf and Western shares control of UIP B.V. with MCA Inc. and MGM/UA Communications Co.

A further difficulty is perhaps posed by the fact that the analysis of external investment in the South African economy has concentrated on those areas of the world where business information is fairly readily available: North America, Western Europe, and the developed countries of the Commonwealth of Nations. Recent international trade statistics indicate, however, that South African trade is expanding rapidly with some countries of Latin America and the east, in particular Argentina,

Brazil, Turkey and Taiwan. Taiwan's exports to South Africa in 1987 were 99% up on the average of its exports in the three years from 1983 to 1985, while its imports from South Africa increased by 146% over the same period (UN 1989a, 7). Some proportion of this expanding trade with relatively new customers persumably represents the fruits of new investment. Thus we learned that Taiwanese banks have financed the establishment in South Africa of joint venture garment manufacturing factories, and that these enterprises have been established under current Taiwanese government policy which encourages investment in employment-intensive manufacturing activities abroad.

Disinvestment by Foreign Companies

Despite these developments it remains true that the principal focus of interest in recent years, and the one that has made the most impact on South African opinion, has been the process of disinvestment in South Africa by foreign companies. The rest of this chapter concentrates on this phenomenon, looking at the purposes, trends, effects and likely future course of disinvestment in the South African economy.

Disinvestment is the withdrawal of foreign companies from their investments, and should be distinguished from divestiture of equities by individuals deciding to sell their shares in South African companies. Disinvestment is very hard to measure. Ideally analysis would take the value of the asset being disposed of as the most important indicator of the process, but business confidentiality, movements in exchange rates, and varying rates of inflation make the generation of reliable measures in a single currency of rates of disinvestment just about impossible to calculate. As guide and illustration, Table 6.1 contains some raw aggregate figures for changes in stocks of capital in South Africa owned by companies in the United States, West Germany and Canada for the fifteen years from 1973 to 1987. These figures are not adjusted for inflation or for the fluctuation in the exchange rate(s) of the Rand, and they do not distinguish between two commonly employed meanings of the term 'capital' – the accumulation of financial resources through deferred consumption, and the physical embodiment of such resources in property of various kinds (factories, equipment, patents, etc.).

What there are data for are the numbers of firms quitting South Africa by selling their equity investments. The figures for the numbers of companies from selected countries taking this course of action up to the end of 1987 and 1988 are set out in Table 6.2. This table includes companies with more than a 10% holding in a South African subsidiary that severed its equity link. Even though the figures do not distinguish between companies that are no more than a two-person telephone answering service and an assembly line employing

Table 6.1   Stocks of Foreign Direct Investment in South Africa, 1973–87

	United States (US$m)	Federal Republic of Germany (DM m)	Canada (Can$m)
1973	1 167	308	104
1974	1 463	419	107
1975	1 583	538	126
1976	1 668	964	126
1977	1 690	804	116
1978	1 851	861	153
1979	1 906	1 164	148
1980	2 350	1 460	141
1981	2 619	1 861	239
1982	2 281	2 095	221
1983	1 987	2 484	213
1984	1 440	2 035	145
1985	1 394	1 182	116
1986	1 567	1 248	200[b]
1987	1 590	[a]	100[b]

[a] 1987 data not yet available.

[b] Preliminary. The apparent increase in 1986 reflects higher retained earnings of some affiliates and possibly one case of temporary reinvestment preparatory to total disinvestment in 1987.

Sources: UN Economic and Social Council, Commission on Transnational Corporations, E/C.10/1989/8, of 14 February 1989, from national data sources.

Code of Conduct: *Canadian Companies in South Africa: Third Annual Report for the Year 1987.*

many hundreds, they are none the less suggestive. By the end of 1988 almost exactly half of the firms from these major countries that had been present in South Africa at the turn of the decade had left. Only one-third of US companies that had been present now remain, and all disinvestment over the twelve months from the end of 1987 to the end of 1988 was even (that is the proportion of all companies remaining in South Africa drawn from each country stayed almost exactly constant). In Switzerland, West Germany and the United Kingdom, where there had formerly been the most reluctance to disinvest, the process seems now to have begun in earnest.

The different patterns of disinvestment between countries reflect different regulatory regimes, as well as different pressures and social forces that are at work from country to country, but they also reflect differences in corporate strategy between firms, and different historical experiences in Africa as a market. Thus, many British companies have a long history in southern Africa, having themselves been a defining part of the British colonial presence there. American investment, on the other hand, and as we have already seen, was relatively recent, and grew most rapidly in the fifteen years from 1966 to 1981. As a result, South African investments tend to be a greater proportion of the global investments of British companies than they are of American companies, which in turn makes the British less inclined to disinvest.

The Investor Responsibility Research Centre (IRRC) in Washington DC has calculated that at the end of 1987 American direct investment in South Africa accounted for less than half a per cent of all American direct investment abroad, and of the 138 American companies surveyed and still present in South Africa, 39 employed fewer than 50 workers, and 72 (52%) fewer than 200. The largest employer, with 2,793 workers of whom 1,588 were black, was the oil company Mobil, which has since announced its intention to disinvest (*Economist*, 5 May 1989). Mobil's assets in South Africa, worth US$400 million, represented less than 1% of its worldwide investments (Cooper 1989, 9, 163–6, 172–3). The relative reluctance of Swiss and West

Table 6.2　Cumulative Disinvestment from South Africa by Country: Numbers of Corporations: end–1987 and end–1988[a]

	Disinvested		Disinvesting		No.		Remaining As % of country's original total		Remaining As % of international total remaining	
	1987	1988	1987	1988	1987	1988	1987	1988	1987	1988
Australia	17	21	–	1	8	8	32	26.6	1.2	1.4
Canada	21	31	3	–	12	6	33	16.25	1.8	1.1
France	6	11	1	–	15	14	68	56.0	2.3	2.5
FRG	10	31	–	1	128	109	93	77.8	19.2	19.2
Netherlands, Norway, Sweden, Denmark	12	23	3	1	27	17	64	41.5	4.1	3.0
Switzerland	2	5	–	–	32	30	94	85.7	4.8	5.3
UK	92	124	7	8	266	225	73	63.0	39.9	39.7
USA	250	293	21	4	178	158	40	34.7	26.7	27.9
TOTAL	410	539	35	15	666	567	60[b]	50.6	100.0	100.1

[a] Counts as a presence in South Africa any holding, directly or indirectly, of equity of more than 10% in a South African affiliate.
[b] That is, of the 1121 foreign corporations originally known to have had equity investments in South Africa, 60% remain.

Source: UN Economic and Social Council, E/1988/23, 8 February 1988; and E/1989/17, 3 March 1989.

German companies to disinvest compared with American companies is also a function of the rather weaker regional and local government pressures for disinvestment in those countries compared with the United States.

The value of the assets that have been disposed of by withdrawing companies is not known, though aggregate figures supplied by the US General Accounting Office show that over the period of their survey, while the number of US companies present in South Africa declined by 30% the value of American direct investment declined by only 10% (US General Accounting Office 1988, 30). None the less, the figures in Table 6.2 do show sharp movements in the value of assets owned by American, West German and Canadian companies, with investment peaking in the years from 1981 to 1983, and falling by half by 1985.

The increases in disinvestment throughout the period from the crisis in 1985 to the end of 1988 reflect four separate but interacting processes. Firstly, lobbying pressures undoubtedly increased during this time, both from anti-apartheid movement supporters in churches, trade unions and race organisations, but also from shareholder and client sources. Business International reported in its *South Africa Alert* publication that the AGMs of US business firms attracted 78 disinvestment motions from the floor in 1986 and 127 such motions in 1987. These experiences interacted with the very high profile that South African social and political developments acquired in the US news media, which brought home to many executives, perhaps for the first time, the squalid nature of apartheid, and the repressive force employed by the regime to maintain its power. Client, shareholder and public pressures were not simply a nuisance, they did also appear to conform with information that company policy-makers were getting from elsewhere. One should never underestimate the importance of the truth.

These factors then also had a bearing on company strategic considerations. The recession in the South African economy in the early 1980s would undoubtedly have encouraged disinvestment by those companies caught in the sectors that were worst hit. In sectors affected by over-supply and the need for structural adjustment, such as the motor-car assembly industry, disinvestment was a rational economic response to a changing business environment. In other sectors, such as the oil industry, where for various reasons having to do with protection and government pricing policies profitability was relatively easy to maintain, disinvestment did not occur.

Fourthly, the changing regulatory environment interacted with each of these three different forces to generate disinvestment responses. The most evident recent example of this is the decision of Mobil to leave South Africa, in response to Congress's 'Rangel Amendment' of December 1987. This requires American companies to pay US taxes on their South African profits as though they were income earned in the US (that is without credit for the taxes they had already paid in South Africa). The change in the law was believed to have cost Mobil US$5 million in 1988. The underlying reason for their decision to withdraw, however, had to do with domestic US market difficulties that senior executives believed would grow if they continued to be present in South Africa. They also took the view that the attitude of Congress towards business or commercial links with South Africa by US firms would continue to harden.

Of the foreign companies that have been, or still are, active in South Africa, in most cases it would be wrong to say that they are there in order to support apartheid, or would leave in order to help to overthrow it. Their main consideration is profitable business, and the decision to depart will finally have been made on an assessment of likely losses arising from poor economic prospects, acute political instability and the threats of possible high costs being incurred from shareholder and client antagonism and consumer resistance.

Anti-apartheid groups have taken the view that disinvestment will hasten the end of apartheid by increasing its isolation from the rest of the world and putting the basis of its economic wealth even more at risk. Disinvestment is also intended to contribute to a diminution of opposition to sanctions by international business interests: the less business they are actually doing in or with South Africa, the less interest they will take.

All businesses, however, are motivated at least in part by an analysis of what the future may be like, and for every company that sees a bleak short-term future for stability in South Africa, there are others which can see attractive opportunities on the horizon. South Africa is not simply the economic giant of southern Africa. It has also, through a combination of geographical circumstance, relative economic stability and a deliberate policy of destabilisation of its neighbours, been able to create a situation in which almost all trade with southern Africa must pass through its ports and transport facilities. International companies regard some kind of presence in the Republic as essential if they are to be able to exploit business opportunities in post-apartheid southern Africa, and with this in mind many are also anxious to sustain good relations with their South African employees and trade unions.

Banks indicated firmly to us that both they and many of their clients now saw South Africa as passing through a transitional phase, one beyond which there would unquestionably be new business opportunities acceptable to Western opinion.

It is also important to recognise that disinvesting companies, especially when driven by the force of opinion, and the propective costs of client and consumer resistance to a continued presence in South Africa, have had to recognise the obligation to try to secure the best return possible for their shareholders from the proceeds of disinvestment. Many have also been influenced by the wish to secure good publicity, both at home and in South Africa itself, for whatever form of disinvestment route was chosen.

Disinvestment has taken four principal and three minor forms (Hauck 1986; Kibbe & Hauck 1988; Anti-Apartheid Movement, London 1988; UN 1989c). Companies either:

(a) sell to South African companies
(b) sell to their own management and/or employees

(c) sell to another foreign company
(d) simply close down.

These four methods of disinvestment accounted for 87% of 115 companies surveyed by the IRRC in 1986 and 1987. Of the remainder, a few either sold or donated their assets to some form of trust; one moved to a neighbouring country (Coca-Cola, which closed its concentrate production facility in Durban and built a new plant in Swaziland, see below) and one gave its assets to a South African church. Companies that were closed accounted for only 11% in the IRRC survey, and they were all small subsidiaries consisting of sales or representative offices with few employees and few physical assets.

The great majority of disinvested businesses were not shut down, and there was no closure or demolition of the physical assets. In most cases the departing company negotiated agreements with the new owners on licensing, servicing, future technology transfers and use of patents and titles, so that the businesses could continue to perform profitably. The one exception appears to have been Kodak, which closed its business down and sold only the equipment, without rights to technology, supplies or industrial secrets. The material was purchased by South African interests and reopened as a going concern, though with only 60% of the former workforce. Executives described the sale as being at 'fire sale prices'. The fact is that the great majority of disinvestment sales have occurred at prices below both the capital value of the assets and the quoted stock exchange price of the companies' shares. Mobil, for instance, is believed to have sold its four South African subsidiaries to Trek, the oil subsidiary of Gencor, for half the book value of the assets. Anglo-American, the big South African conglomerate, acquired another 18% of the shares in Samcor, the vehicle-assembly business that was previously jointly owned by the Ford Motor Company, for what Ford described as a 'nominal' sum.

The actual method of disinvestment chosen by departing companies is a reflection of what they believe to be most important. The most popular option has been to sell to a South

African company, but although this may maximise the sale price it has the disadvantageous effect of leaving the seller to export the proceeds through the financial Rand exchange rate, thereby taking a further loss of perhaps up to 40%. It is this prospect which has made the negotiation of leasing arrangements and other special contracts so popular, since the income and profits from these deals will be paid in commercial Rand.

Similar considerations have prompted management buy-outs (MBOs) of the self-financing variety, where the disinvestor lends the managers the funds for the purchase and then imposes conditions on the company's activities while the loan is outstanding. MBOs also have the effect of ensuring management continuity, the maximum opportunity to maintain market share, and the possibility of a repurchase option for the disinvestor to return to a post-apartheid South Africa. These advantages have had to be balanced against the fact that MBOs always involve the seller receiving a lower price than it would have received in a public offer of sale.

Selling to another foreign company has not been a very attractive proposition because most companies, even in countries with long histories of a presence in South Africa, if they are currently asking themselves any questions at all, are wondering whether they should leave, and not whether they should get further in. The result is that the market is very depressed, and the price likely to be obtained correspondingly poor. The advantage of such a sale is, of course, that some part at least of the payment may be made in a currency other than Rand, so that the proceeds will not have to be brought out through the financial Rand. It is worth mentioning, in this regard, that the financial Rand is responsive to the news of further asset sales by foreign companies inside South Africa. Simply the news of Mobil's sale to Trek drove the financial Rand down by 1.2%.

The use of trusts for disinvestment has included many different purposes. For some the intention is to evade anti-apartheid laws or regulations, for instance by establishing a trust in an off-shore haven, and then lending the trust money to purchase the assets of the company, which is thus being disinvested only in the most nominal sense.

Others have sought to find a way out of South Africa that would preserve a corporate image and continue over at least the medium term to protect and advance certain corporate interests. A good example of this is provided by the Ford Motor Company's plan for disinvestment. Through its Canadian subsidiary Ford owned 42% of the shares of Samcor, a motor-vehicle company formed in 1985 by a merger between Ford and Amcar, a South African company owned by Anglo-American Corporation. Under an agreement negotiated between Ford, Anglo-American, and the National Union of Metalworkers of South Africa (Numsa), 24 of these 42% were donated to a worker-managed trust and the remainder sold to Anglo-American for a nominal sum. The trust was to have seven trustees, all employees of Samcor, five elected by hourly-paid employees and two by salaried employees (reflecting the proportions of the workforce as a whole). Dividends paid to the trust were to be distributed to development projects throughout South Africa, as chosen by the trustees. Ford's disinvestment was completed at the end of April 1988. In negotiating the agreement Numsa declined an offer that dividends should be distributed directly to employees, but this arrangement subsequently became a matter of controversy among workers, leading to a strike at the Samcor Pretoria plant in mid-April 1988 (Kibbe & Hauck 1988, 38–41). There were claims that workers had not been adequately consulted about the deal, and suggestions that workers would prefer either to have the dividends paid to them annually, or the shares sold and the capital sum dispersed to them immediately. At least some of this controversy may have been related to inter-union rivalries. Under a provision of the trust which allowed changes to the deed amenable to the beneficiaries, it was subsequently decided that the dividends of the trust would be awarded to the company's employees. This decision, taken eight days after the strike action had started, brought factory operations back to normal.

In addition to what can only be described as giving away its assets in South Africa, when Ford announced its plans to disinvest it also injected a further US$61 million into Samcor to retire debt and enable the company to retool. The Ford company currently donates US$250,000 a year to a program to enable black workers to train for management positions in Samcor at Ford plants outside South Africa, a sum in excess of the US$200,000 per annum which it reports receiving from Samcor in licensing and trademark fees. Ford of Canada is also committed to donating approximately US$10 million to three separate educational and community trusts in South Africa.

The IRRC lists 151 American and Canadian companies which, in the wake of disinvestment, have preserved non-equity links with South African business operations. These vary from the simplest possible arrangement, such as that of Trans World Airlines, which closed its offices in South Africa in 1985 and now markets tickets through an agency on commission, to Coca-Cola, which sells the concentrate from its new plant in Swaziland to independent bottlers and retailers in South Africa who are licensed to use the trade mark. In setting up this arrangement, Coca-Cola sold its South African assets to a company called National Beverage Service Industries (Pty) Ltd (NBS) under terms that involved the leasing of franchises and the sale of 9% of the company's equity to bottlers and small retailers, and the sale of a further 2% of Coca-Cola shares to employees of the company. Coca-Cola told the IRRC that three-quarters of the shareholders who purchased shares, and 60% of the franchised retailers, are black. NBS is responsible for the use and protection of the Coca-Cola trademark, and for marketing, technical support and quality control for the independent franchised bottlers and canners. Coca-Cola also reported that 51% of the equity in their former bottling plant in East London is now owned by Kilimanjaro Investments, a company formed by black South African investors. Kilimanjaro bought 49% of the equity in the plant in March 1987, but had to wait another thirteen months to get the government approval that is necessary for blacks to have

majority ownership of business enterprises in white areas
(Kibbe & Hauck 1988, 13–14).

It is important not to get examples of this kind out of
proportion. The overwhelming majority of black people in
South Africa live in conditions of poverty of Third World
standards and the number who are in a position to participate
in capital ownership is infinitesimally small. Nor have the
opportunities been numerous. We give these examples simply
in order to illustrate the range of possibilities that exist in the
field of disinvestment.

Within the range embraced by the examples we have given,
we can say that non-equity links have evolved to serve three
broad purposes: they preserve a presence and provide for a
stream of investment income from South Africa; they probably
enable the sale to take place at a higher price, because they
preserve both technological co-operation and the presence of
the trademark, which help to maximise the economic value of
the assets, and they provide a means whereby the disinvestor
can retreive some of its investment through fees paid at the
higher commercial Rand exchange rate. In this last matter,
however, and as we saw earlier, the SARB preserves an interest
in deciding whether licence and franchise 'fees' might not more
appropriately be termed 'capital' and relegated to the financial
Rand exchange rate.

There is no comprehensive evidence on how much Western
companies extract from the South African economy in non-
equity investment fees, but it must be remembered that
licensing and franchising is a common and worldwide phenomenon of contemporary capitalism that would, surely, pass
without notice in South Africa (as it does everywhere else) had
it not become visible as an element associated with disinvestment strategies brought about by the existence of apartheid.
What they do do, however, is to reduce the cost to the South
African economy of disinvestment decisions by preserving
access to current technology, future development and best
practice management techniques, without which, even though
sold originally as going concerns, the disinvested companies

would fall behind foreign standards of performance and profitability. Against this view, which seems to us unexceptionable, it can be argued that the preservation of licensing and franchise links provides foreign companies with the opportunity to continue to exercise leverage over management conduct, particularly with regard to personnel and employment issues, over their former companies. The debate about the propriety of licensing links by foreign companies to a South Africa that is still governed by the regime of apartheid is only now just beginning (Kibbe and Hauck 1988, 25–34). However, the South African government is already preparing for the possibility that foreign firms will be pressured into unilateral termination of licence, trademark and technical agreements. A Protection of Businesses Amendment Bill, introduced into parliament in mid-April 1989 contains provisions designed to protect South African companies from legal action in South African courts by giving the Minister of Economic Affairs the power to decide when licensing agreements should be cancelled (*Business International*, May 1989). It is hard to see how the legislation can be made to work, however.

In the meantime, we may best summarise the economic effects of disinvestment in the following way:

1 Disinvestment has had almost no impact on South Africa's balance of payments situation since the dual exchange rate was reintroduced in 1985. The sale of assets and repatriation abroad of the proceeds necessarily passes via the financial Rand, where it neither pressurises the current-account surpluses nor draws down the foreign reserves. It simply, as with the case of Mobil mentioned earlier, drives down the exchange rate of the financial Rand. This fact has led to the negotiation of licensing and franchising arrangements which enable fees to be repatriated through the higher commercial Rand, but these do not put additional pressure on the balance of payments in any greater degree than the dividends and profits from the investments which were formerly paid in this way.

2 Disinvestment has certainly contributed to a climate of

uncertainty in South African business which is one reason for the increasingly audible calls from the business sector for accelerated social, economic and political reform. It is always difficult to measure, and sometimes even to define 'business confidence', but the rapid departure of so many and in most cases highly 'visible' foreign undertakings, though it has enabled some cheap acquisitions, must also have had a destabilising effect.

3 Disinvestment has altered the composition and direction of savings and investment flows in South Africa, diverting domestic funds from new investment opportunities at a time when South Africa, because of its exclusion from international capital markets, is being forced to rely on its own resources for new development. This is probably one (though only one) of the reasons for the very slow pace of the government's privatisation program, which has now been stalled for over a year.

4 Despite the proliferation of licensing agreements between disinvesting firms and their purchasers, technological and management links with the West have none the less been weakened in some degree. This weakening is bound to have consequences for the efficient functioning of firms at the micro level, and will therefore lead in due course to the further misallocation of resources at a time when the economy is already badly in need of reform for precisely this reason.

5 Disinvestment has reduced foreign business stakes in South Africa and therefore has reduced their immediate interest in, if not apartheid, at least social and political stability. A decline in direct interest in the future of the Republic is of some considerable importance in political systems that give substantial room for lobbying. Thus, whereas a large enterprise with substantial interests in South Africa might devote considerable resources to lobbying Congressmen to try to ensure that legislation does not adversely affect its interests there, once it has disinvested and severed its links with South Africa it will

cease to take the same interest. Indeed it may even, rather like the reformed smoker, begin to take the other side of the argument altogether.

6 There are the economic consequences for the non-white majority population of South Africa. Here the debate will need to be in possession of rather more information than is currently at our disposal. Unemployment arising from disinvestment appears to have been modest, but we have only fragmentary quantitative data. Arthur D. Little, the firm of consultants responsible for monitoring and reporting on the adherence of US companies to the Statement of Principles for South Africa (previously known as the Sullivan Code) said that only one of the companies that was disinvested during 1986 and 1987 remained a signatory of the principles once ownership had changed hands. However, some have stated publicly their intention to continue to apply the principles. The aspects of the principles thought most likely to suffer by neglect are Principles VI and VII – 'improving the quality of employees' lives outside the work environment in such areas as housing, transportation, schooling, recreation and health facilities' and 'working to eliminate laws and customs which impede social, economic and political justice' – which were affordable by large foreign multinational corporations and may not be by local purchasers. Against this, the franchise and licence arrangements contracted for by some disinvestors may be creating opportunities for non-white business people.

7 Perhaps the most important economic consequence of disinvestment is the poor outlook that it is creating for new current and future foreign investment in South Africa. The departure of so many important international companies is sure to be discouraging other firms from pursuing new investment opportunities in South Africa and is itself putting pressure on those foreign firms which are still there to contemplate leaving. In addition, though the disinvesting firms are not removing the physical assets or, in some cases, the technology and know-how, nor by returns are they investing

in new plant and machinery, or ensuring that their former South African subsidiaries are in a position to play a leading role in the South African market of the future. These costs will have to be borne by the South African economy in due course, and it is here, in the future, that disinvestment is contributing to South Africa's problem with capital flows. This is one reason why the Ford Company's decision to inject US$61 million into its former South African subsidiary even as it left, aroused such controversy, since it was putting off the day when the full effects of its departure would have to be met. The transfer eventually required the authorisation of the Office of Foreign Assets Control of the US Department of the Treasury.

In conclusion, however, it must be emphasised that South Africa's problems with capital flows are most acute not as a result of disinvestment by foreign firms, but as a result of the breakdown of South Africa's relationship with the international financial community.

The pressure on its balance of payments, and on the future of its potential rate of growth on which depends its capacity to generate new employment opportunities, derives from its exclusion from the world stock of savings. The climate of uncertainty and anxiety that this exclusion, quite rightly, generates in political, business and commercial circles in South Africa, will in turn have effects on overall economic performance. If this performance is poor, which seems to us to be likely, then this in turn will lead to further disinvestment by foreign companies, and a further degradation of local confidence. This is because our analysis suggests that those firms which disinvest do so under the pressure both of losses in a declining or over-supplied South African market, and the effects of heavy lobbying and pressures on them in Western markets which are of value to them. The balance of these influences varies from case to case, but it is the combination which matters. The pressures required to remove a company from a highly profitable South African market are different from, and more intense than, the pressures required to get a foreign firm to disinvest from an unprofitable or marginal South African market. If a company still sees its presence in South Africa as a component in its global or regional future operations, then it is more likely to persist at least until the local economic climate has deteriorated rather further.

It is persistence with apartheid, and the embargo on international financial flows, which are going to bring this about.

CHAPTER SEVEN

Gold

It is a conventional wisdom that South Africa is safe from complete isolation by the West because of its gold and mineral wealth. Precious stones, minerals of great strategic importance and rarity, and the bulk of the Western world's supplies of gold, mean that whatever Western leaders might say about South Africa they will always do enough to ensure its survival.

Though this issue is of great moment, our interest here is not in tradeable commodities, whether of ultimately frivolous items such as diamonds, or essential and strategic ones such as vanadium, but with the international financial system, and its links with apartheid. In this context gold is of considerable interest.

Until 1971, with its price fixed at US$35 an ounce, gold performed the function of a reserve currency. Since the collapse of the post-war international monetary system, and the development of a free gold market, it has continued to play a role, though a declining one, in the reserves of all the central banks of the developed world. It has also become a haven for certain investors at various times, acting almost as a barometer of confidence in economic and political stability. Gold, while being a primary commodity with industrial uses and applications in manufacturing, is also widely seen as a currency, an investment offering capital gains, a hedge against fluctuations in exchange rates and rates of inflation, and a 'last resort' investment against political, social or economic catastrophe. It also appears still to be of social importance in some countries, where it may be perceived as having emotional significance of bizarre, almost quasi-magical dimensions.

For South Africa gold has served as the guarantor of white prosperity and stability. Without its gold exports South Africa would run unsustainable deficits on its external account, would have failed to attract investment, and been unable to diversify its economy. It is on the basis of the mineral extraction industries that there evolved the system of migrant labour, with its fundamental principle that black male workers left home, without their wives and families, to live and work at the mines. Alongside the segregation and racial mistrust of this system grew the institutionalisation of racism in the labour market, white unionised labour fighting for a superior position in a divided labour force and eventually forging a political coalition of interest with white racism in the society as a whole (Lanning & Mueller 1979, 154–67; Lipton, 1985, 110–37, 183–226). Gold mining, though as we shall see in decline, still employs more than half a million workers.

In the course of its development gold mining has emerged as an oligopoly. The two great phases of investment and increased production in the industry, the first at the turn of the century and the second in the years after the Second World War, saw the emergence of seven mining houses, controlled by only four conglomerate companies, which dominate the industry. They are a major force in the whole South African economy, financing investment in manufacturing and mining industries generally, and in the strategically important field of extracting oil from coal. As disinvestment by foreign companies has gathered pace in recent years, it is the gold conglomerates that have been able to snap up investment opportunities at cheap prices. In the past decade they have also been keen to diversify their holdings and activities abroad, partly in order to consolidate their position in the world gold market, partly as a pre-emptive manoeuvre against future possible sanctions, and partly as a hedge against the possibility of traumatic and disruptive domestic change.

Historically the three largest of the South African gold-mining companies have accounted for approximately 60% of the gold production of the Western world.

This enormous financial and economic strength is now showing signs of ebbing away, however. Figures for world gold supply are set out in Table 7.1

In the past decade world gold supplies have risen by 76%, going up from 1,301 tonnes in 1980 to an estimated 2,290 in 1989. South Africa's share of this total production has fallen from 52% to 27.5%. As a percentage of the Western world's production, South Africa's decline has also been sharp, going from just over 70% in 1980 to a forecast of just under 40% in the current year. And the decline has not only been relative, it is also absolute. The peak of production was reached in 1970, when South Africa produced a thousand tonnes, since when it has (with tiny fluctuations) been in continuous decline.

With the rapid increase in gold supplies from other quarters, gold production is now highly competitive. Whereas in 1980 the Western world outside South Africa produced about 284 tonnes, by 1987 it had increased this to 766 tonnes: an increase of 270%. In the medium term this rate of increase may continue. Table 7.2 shows the gold production of South Africa's main competitors in the Western world over three recent years.

In the three most recent years the gold-mine production of Canada, the United States and Australia combined has risen from being 47% of South Africa's production to being almost 80% – and it is still rising, and rising rapidly, as the output of new investment comes on stream.

The world market for gold is so peculiar that it is hard to say whether this increased supply is in response to an increased demand in any conventional economic sense. 'Consumption' appears to have increased, but much of this consumption must of necessity have been occurring through hoarding. In Table 7.3 we set out the figures for total world gold 'demand' over the past three years.

Table 7.1 World Gold Supplies, 1980–89 (tonnes)

	1980	1981	1982	1983	1984	1985	1986	1987	1988(a)	1989(b)
1 Mine production in the non-communist world	959	981	1 028	1 115	1 160	1 233	1 291	1 373	1 500	1 590
2 Net communist sales	90	280	203	93	205	210	402	303	300	350
3 Net official sales(c) (purchases)	(230)	(276)	(85)	142	85	(135)	(143)	(70)	(200)	(100)
4 Gold loan forward sales	–	–	–	–	–	–	–	80	200	100
5 Scrap	482	232	237	289	284	299	465	402	300	350
A TOTAL SUPPLY	1 301	1 217	1 383	1 639	1 734	1 607	2 015	2 088	2 100	2 290
6 Production in South Africa	675	658	664	680	683	673	640	607	616	630
7 Share of South Africa's production in production of non-communist world (6 ÷ 1)%	70.4	67.0	64.6	61.0	58.9	54.6	49.6	44.1	41.1	39.6
8 Share of South Africa's production in world supply (6 ÷ A)%	51.9	54.0	48.0	41.5	39.4	41.9	31.8	29.0	29.3	27.5

(a) Estimated.
(b) Forecasts.
(c) Central banks and government-controlled investment agencies.

Source: Consolidated Gold Fields Plc.

Table 7.2   Western Gold Production by Country, 1986–88 (tonnes)

	1986	1987	1988[a]
South Africa	640	607	616
USA	118	155	190
Canada	106	120	145
Australia	75	108	155
Papua New Guinea	36	34	32
Brazil	67	84	90
Other Latin America	107	107	105
Philippines	39	40	37
Other	103	118	130
TOTAL	1 291	1 373	1 500

[a] Estimated.
Source: Consolidated Gold Fields Plc.

Table 7.3   World Gold Demand, 1986–88 (tonnes)

	1986	1987	1988
Manufacturing			
Jewellery	1 104	1 138	1 350
Electronics	124	124	120
Dentistry	51	48	40
Other industrial	68	72	70
TOTAL	1 347	1 382	1 580
World supply	2 015	2 088	2 100
Surplus	668	706	520
Hoarding			
Gold coins	327	207	120
Gold bars	341	499	400

Source: Consolidated Gold Fields Plc.

While industrial consumption of gold has remained fairly constant over the past three years, worldwide gold demand for the jewellery industry has increased by a little over 22%. Despite this increase the surge in gold supplies is generating huge surpluses which, in a declining market for gold coins, appears to have been going into gold-bar hoarding. Gold refineries report long waiting lists for gold bars, and with world gold supplies forecast to increase by a further 9% in 1989, it seems likely that hoarding of this character may well account for anything from 500 to 620 tonnes in the current year.

It is a commonplace in the West to imagine that gold consumption is a phenomenon of affluence. The Italian jewellery industry, which purchases approximately 100 tonnes of South African-produced gold a year, and which is the largest Western 'consumer' for this purpose, recently attracted a certain amount of adverse publicity as a result of this fact (World Gold Commission 1988; *Financial Mail*, 9 December 1988; *Metal Bulletin*, 6 February 1989; *Guardian*, 9 March 1989). In fact, the greatest increases in gold 'consumption' have been coming not from the affluent countries of the West, but from the rapidly growing economies of Asia. Table 7.4 gives the figures for the two most recent years.

Table 7.4   Gold Demand in Asia: Principal Markets, 1987–88 (tonnes)

	1987	1988 [a]
Japan	240	270
Hong Kong	177	390
Singapore	28	150
Taiwan	191	200
India [a]	105	150
TOTAL	741	1 160
As % of total world supplies	35.5	55.2

[a] Estimates: the figures in the 1988 column are real consumption figures for January–October, plus an estimate for the final two months of the year.
Source: Consolidated Gold Fields Plc.

As Table 7.4 shows, Asian demand accounted for more than half of total world demand in 1988, and this demand was itself a massive 56.5% greater than it had been the previous year. Experts in the industry believe that this is a reflection of two separate phenomena: first, the strengthening value of Asian currencies, particularly of the yen, which is making gold a progressively 'cheaper' investment, and secondly, that Asian consumers of gold respond more readily to price signals than Western consumers do, so that when gold is cheap they will purchase more, and vice versa. One South African expert has described this, optimistically, as 'providing a floor to the gold price by acting contra-cyclically to the Western investor' (Brown 1989a).

In reality much of the emergence of the Asian market seems to us to have to do with institutional factors. Certainly the continuous long-term appreciation of the yen is one crucial element. Another is the approach of 1997 in Hong Kong, which is precisely the kind of political development that leads to investor gold hoarding. In addition, Hong Kong's role as an international centre of investment and trade almost certainly means that many of the purchases made there are in fact for a Japanese and Chinese clientele. Furthermore, increased consumption in Taiwan has been government led in the sense that Taiwan:

(a) recently relaxed its laws prohibiting the private ownership of gold, and

(b) through the Taiwan Reserve Bank, has entered the gold market as a major purchaser for its reserves.

These purchases would, apparently, have been even greater had it not been for the restraining influence of the United States, which has reportedly put pressure on Taiwan to slow its program of acquisition (Brown 1988, 7).

In the South African gold-mining industry, where the appearance of an Asian market has seemed to offer a life-line to a profitable present, if not a secure future, they describe this new Asian market as the 'gold sponge', a term that offers almost limitless opportunites for mixed metaphor. Thus 'the ingestion capacity of the Oriental gold sponge should be one of the keys to future gold price behaviour' (Brown ibid.).

Will it be? Table 7.5 gives the average price for gold measured in US dollars and in SDRs, along with the high and low points in each year.

Since the heady days of the post oil-shocks gold markets, when the price per ounce was poised near the US$1,000 mark, the market price has both fallen and become somewhat less volatile. Measured in Special Drawing Rights – that is, more or

Table 7.5   Annual Average Gold Price, 1980–88[a] (US$ per ounce & SDRs)

| | US$ | | | SDRs | | |
	Max.	Min.	Average	Max.	Min.	Average
1980	843.00	474.00	608.37	–	–	–
1981	599.25	391.75	459.63	–	–	–
1982	488.50	297.00	376.32	450.77	273.61	341.45
1983	511.50	207.13	422.38	469.83	191.91	394.95
1984	406.85	303.25	360.45	381.50	307.56	351.09
1985	339.30	284.00	317.47	343.45	290.43	312.47
1986	442.75	326.00	367.83	365.03	285.79	312.84
1987	493.90	392.60	447.00	378.56	311.20	345.34
1988	485.30	389.05	437.04	364.85	302.53	325.16

[a] New York prices. The average is derived from daily figures throughout the year.

Source: Reuters Money Market Rates and Mineral Databases.

less completely eliminating the effects of currency fluctuations – we can see that the average annual price from 1982 to 1988 did not fluctuate outside the band from 300 to 400, and that for most of that time the average SDR price lay in the band from 310 to 350.

In US dollar terms, however, the trends look rather different. In the second half of 1987 the price lay between US$440 and $490 an ounce. In the first eight months of 1988 it slipped to between US$430 and $460. On 12 September it went below US$420, and nine days later to below $400. More recently, in the second quarter of 1989, it sat in the band from $370 to $390 before slipping below $360 on 22 May. Even industry analysts are not optimistic that the downward drift in the dollar price has yet come to an end. That gold did not appreciate substantially in price in the wake of the stock-market adjustment in 1987 is a factor contributing to this view. In the absence of serious and prolonged international crises – which probably would influence the price upwards again – it is difficult to disagree.

A number of different factors are influencing this decline, and they are worth setting out in a little detail because they have important implications for the argument which is to follow.

First, there has been a return to relative stability in international currency markets. Some of this has been managed, in the sense that central banks have in recent years played a more concerted role in seeking currency alignments that more closely reflect the true 'worth' of a currency in terms of its trade and balance of payments situation.

Second, central banks have started to manage their reserves in a more innovative and interventionist way than was the case even in the recent past. With the emergence of the multicurrency reserve asset system (Pringle 1982) central banks have diversified their holdings and sought to preserve their value and/or improve the return that can be made available from them by investment. None sees any future in a return to gold as the international reserve standard and many now see it as at most a residual component in central bank portfolios. As one bank expressed it to the Group of Thirty study in 1982: 'The main problem is how to mobilise gold in case of need without affecting the private markets'. In the past three years 'mobilising gold' does appear to have become a small part of central bank asset management. Central banks are conservative in the mix of assets that they hold, but all have become concerned at how the capital value of their gold assets has been falling as the price declines, and that since the gold that they hold is not put to any productive purpose they are not achieving an investment return either. This perception has led to the recent innovation of gold 'loans' whereby gold is lent to manufacturers for short-term periods in return for interest payments. It has also led to some central banks reducing the proportion of their reserves that they hold in gold, and there have been notable cases recently of banks selling sizeable portions of their gold stocks on the open market. The most recent was Belgium, which sold approximately US$1.7 billion of gold in March 1989. In other words, though it is difficult to mobilise gold without affecting the private markets, there is evidence to show that this is an aspect of asset management which central banks are now mastering. As another part of this same development, buying and selling forward have also started to feature as more common practices that may also be conducive of stability.

As well as the management of reserves, the steady decline in the price of gold is also believed to reflect other aspects of macroeconomic management in the Western world. These include:

- low rates of inflation in the OECD countries, which despite slight upward movements in the past twelve months in the United States and the United Kingdom, look set to stay moderate in the medium term;
- relatively high interest rates that provide opportunities for investment that are far more attractive than gold, which has not been appreciating in capital value and can provide no interest return for the small- and medium-sized investors;
- a renewal of interest in alternative investments with high capital gain potential, such as real estate;
- the expansion of the gold-mining industry itself, outside South Africa, which has had a strong attraction for equity investors (that is they now buy gold-mining shares rather than coin and bullion).

These factors together, steadily lowering the price in a context of relative stability, are having a particularly damaging effect on the South African gold-mining industry and its prospects. This is largely because of the cost structure of the industry.

The rise of gold production in the rest of the world has been facilitated by new methods of mining, a higher strike rate in prospecting with more accurate methods of load factor forecasting, and the introduction of new low-cost technology. The South African industry has so far been able to draw only limited benefits from these developments.

One reason for this is the declining grades of ore being mined. South Africa's mines are relatively old, and some are near the end of their working lives. The deterioration of grade per tonne milled has been marked in recent years, going from 8.85 grams per tonne in 1985 to 5.08 grams per tonne in September 1988 (Brown 1989b). Part of the explanation for this change has to do with devaluation, and its interaction with government regulations that govern the conduct of the mining companies. As the value of the Rand has fallen internationally, so the Rand price of gold has risen, which in turn lowers the pay limit of economically exploitable ore. But this development cannot account for all of the sharp alteration in the grade per tonne milled. The underlying reality is that the older mines, seriously depleted, are now offering only lower-grade ores from less-uniform reefs, and in an effort to maintain output the companies are having to raise the tonnages milled to compensate for the unpredictable yields.

This has further exacerbated another development to which it is allied. South African gold mines are deep, some of them down to 4,000 metres, and the costs of keeping these difficult enterprises functioning is constantly rising. In March 1989 it was estimated that almost 8% of South Africa's current gold production was, at the then price, being produced at a loss, and a further 18% was marginal. This production comes from twenty-two of the forty-three gold mines in South Africa. A further reduction in the world price to say a band of between US$330 and $360 would mean that all twenty-two of them would be running at a loss, and could only continue to maintain production with a further, drastic, devaluation of the Rand.

Although devaluation has the effect of sustaining company revenues in the short term, making them continue to appear profitable, it also places yet further pressure on their cost structure by raising input prices from imports, and contributing to increased labour costs due to inflation.

Companies have dealt with the emergence of these linked problems in a number of different ways. Some have invested in the new technologies of trackless mechanical mining and longwalling, but in the deep and difficult environment of the older mines this has been a factor contributing to grade erosion. (The machines are less selective than humans, so greater tonnages are milled for the same output.) Other companies have cut capital expenditure as part of an attempt to cut costs in general, which can only serve as a short-term expedient. Thus even Free State Consolidated, which with production of

104,364 kilograms in 1988 is South Africa's single largest producer, recently announced that it was to cut its planned capital expenditure program by almost 50% (*Financial Mail*, 7 April 1989).

All the mining companies are engaging in new prospecting and there are strong hopes in the industry that the opportunity exists for a third wave of expansion in the last decade of the century. Hopes currently focus on the land around the perimeter of the central Rand basin, with particular interest in the southern Orange Free State, the Bothaville Gap, the Klerksdorp and Potchefstroom Gap region, the far west Rand, and the Evander area. Even so, it is widely believed that some feasibility studies in these areas reveal only relatively low grade ores at considerable depths, and the development costs of these projects are very high. One expert has calculated that the fifteen new gold-mining projects that could be launched by the turn of the century would have a combined capital cost of 28.3 billion Rand (Brown 1989b, 14–15).

Conscious of the importance of launching a new phase of investment, the government appointed a technical committee on mining taxation (the Marais Committee) to recommend a new taxation regime that would encourage further investment. The committee's report recently recommended such proposals as the phasing out of current tax surcharges; much accelerated depreciation of capital expenditure (100% redemption in the year incurred); and a phasing out of lease payments for existing producers. Even with the adoption of these proposals, however, the viability of the great majority of the envisaged new gold mining ventures is dependent on a Rand gold price in excess of current market values.

The cost problems of the South African gold-mining industry, both now and in the immediate future, look decidedly worse in the context of production elsewhere in the world. Measured in US dollars, South African production costs per ounce of gold moved from $189 in 1985, when it ranked first in the world, to $261 in 1987, when it ranked fifth behind Canada, the United States, the Philippines and Australia.

Although these figures are a little misleading, in the sense that they reflect exchange rate fluctuations as well as real movements in the relative cost structures of the various industries, what they do mean is that South Africa is in no position to compete with other producers by adopting an aggressive marketing policy.

A falling price, ageing mines, depleting reserves, declining grades, a rising cost structure, high capital requirements to finance a new generation of mines, potentially difficult mining conditions in the new mines even if the international price of gold recovers: the situation facing South Africa's gold-mining industry is not yet one of crisis, but it is of deep current concern in white South Africa.

The concern is linked, naturally, to the central role that gold plays in the South African economy. In 1988 gold accounted for 38.4% of all South African export earnings. It accounts for almost one-eighth of GDP and 10% of all government revenues. Although precise figures for the contribution of the gold sector to South African savings are not available, its contribution is certainly highly significant, because gold is such an important segment of the corporate sector which in turn accounts for the bulk of South Africa's domestic savings.

Of the more than 600 tonnes of gold that are mined in South Africa every year, hardly two or three tonnes are absorbed by the local South African market for carat jewellery and dentistry. The international trade in Kruggerrands, which by the early 1980s absorbed about 100 tonnes of South African gold, has been virtually eliminated by the international embargo. As a result, all gold exports from South Africa take the form of pure gold ingots. The strictly controlled and regulated industry is required to sell its gold to the South African Reserve Bank within one month of production, and receives payment in Rand. The SARB is responsible for marketing the gold internationally.

Information about the countries and companies which purchase gold from South Africa has not been made publicly available in recent years. 'The world of gold', as one banker expressed it to us, 'is very small and rather private. It is hard to know what goes on'. None the less, one recent analysis (Koistinen and Lind 1988) estimated that in 1985, 121 tonnes of South African gold went to Italy, 205 tonnes went through the London market, and 308 tonnes through Zurich. Only 31 tonnes of gold was imported by other countries directly from South Africa. (The figures for Asian gold purchases given in Table 7.4 should make for caution in assuming that this situation remains unchanged in 1989.) In Zurich the Union Bank of Switzerland, the Swiss Bank Corporation and the Credit Suisse together form a pool which controls the gold market, including the almost 50% of South African production which they take. In London the gold market is similarly dominated by a small number of banks from different countries, which set the price twice a day and ensure orderly dealing.

Given the known quantities of production, and the small number of institutions that are involved in the gold trade with South Africa, it is unsurprising that suggestions should have developed for a sanction to be directed at South African gold exports. This proposal appears even more attractive in the light of its critical importance to the South African economy as a whole. If South Africa could no longer sell its gold on the international market its economy would, at least in the short to medium term, be wrecked.

Gold differs from many other tradeable commodities exported by South Africa in three crucial ways, however, and these differences place grave difficulties in the path of a successful sanction. First, gold – even at today's depressed price – is a very high-value item per unit of weight. It is relatively easily moved, can be melted and cast into any shape or form, and would pose few difficulties for those already experienced in devising ways around embargoes and blockades.

Secondly, compared with other South African exports which are the subject of sanctions and which in terms of the quantities involved are of lesser importance on international markets (e.g.

coal and steel), South African gold amounts to a significant proportion of all gold available on the world market. Even in the context of a declining share of the market, rising costs, and relatively low rates of return, South African gold still accounted for nearly 30% of worldwide supply and 40% of the supply from Western countries in 1988. South Africa remains the largest single producer and supplier of gold to world markets. Any successful sanction has, therefore, to be introduced in the knowledge that it is going to cause major disruption to the world market in gold, and that this disruption will have important implications for the price.

Several proposals have been made in recent years to try to take account of this fact, and to neutralise it. More than ten years ago it was suggested that central banks should simply offload their stocks of gold onto the world market, thereby depressing the price as a means of ruining the South African industry. More recently it has been suggested (Salant 1988) that the United States should, of its own accord, simply announce the following policy: 'As of some specified future date, the US Treasury stands ready – for a specified limited time – both to sell gold and to buy gold from anyone at the specified reduced price'. According to this idea, the announcement itself would have the effect of bringing the price of gold down to the level specified, because traders would sell in order to avoid future capital losses. The American authorities might even undertake some actual sales, should it prove necessary to demonstrate the firmness of the intention, but the probability is that the expectation of sales would suffice to set in motion the appropriate chain of rational responses to the expectation. The author of this proposal argues that 'unlike trade restrictions on exports to or imports from South Africa, which can in principle – and have in practice – been easily circumvented by shipping through intermediaries, there is no way to evade this sanction'.

It is certainly the case that Fort Knox contains supplies of gold such that, were the United States Federal Reserve to threaten to enter the world market as a principal supplier, it could reasonably expect to set the price. This is also true of most of the other advanced industrialised countries. Of the total estimated world stocks of gold of 90,000 to 100,000 tonnes, nearly 35,600 tonnes are held by central banks, the International Monetary Fund, the European Monetary Co-operation Fund and the Bank for International Settlements. The remainder, perhaps 60% of the total, is in private hands. Gold belonging to the industrial countries and to the IMF amounts to 30,700 tonnes, which is the equivalent of over fifteen years of current levels of world gold production and twenty years of current demand for jewellery and all other industrial and commercial uses. Measured at the price of gold in December 1987, the value of these stocks was close to US$475 billion. At $300 an ounce the reserves would still have a combined value of roughly $300 billion, while the value of all the gold (excluding scrap) absorbed by the private market in 1987 amounted to 'only' $24 billion.

These figures are indicative. Sufficient stocks of gold exist for the market to be depressed if there was the will among the monetary authorities of the industrialised countries (governments, central banks, treasuries, etc.) to pursue such a strategy.

This fact is of relevance to another proposal about South African gold that has recently been advanced by a group calling itself the World Gold Commission. This London-based body, which was set up on the initiative of anti-apartheid organisations, has a research program that is funded by the United Nations Centre on Apartheid. They argue (World Gold Commission 1989?) that an effective sanction on gold from South Africa could be imposed country by country, as long as those who imposed it also pursued a strategy of releasing from reserves onto the market each year an amount of gold equivalent to what would have been purchased from South Africa. Sales of this kind, they believe, would have the effect of keeping the price stable (or at least of preventing it from fluctuating more than it otherwise would) while also providing a significant benefit for the countries which pursue the objective: namely that they would convert more of their unproductive gold reserves into currency, which could then be deployed in the form of interest-bearing securities. The sales of gold would have the effect not only of preventing the price of gold rising on the open market, but also of preventing South Africa from profiting from the higher price brought about by increased scarcity.

This superficially appealing proposal has a number of damaging weaknesses. By no means all holders of gold reserves are agreed about their limited utility. As we have seen, some countries like Taiwan are now entering the market as major new purchasers of bullion for reserve purposes, a development that suggests that some authorities attach considerable importance to their gold holdings. Furthermore, though the intention of the proposal is for the gold price to be kept stable, the actual achievement of this objective would in practice be very difficult. The market would certainly interpret movements in price as indicative of central bank sale interventions, and it is notoriously true that official moves to influence markets are more readily provocative of instability than stability. A sharp fall in the price of gold has an immediate impact on the value of everybody's reserves, whether they are being held by industrial or developing countries. It is not the intended outcome of the proposal, but intervention could, in this way, seriously undermine the economic and political stability of third-party countries themselves in a fragile state of development. It would also affect the revenues of gold-producing countries, where it would be sure to incur hostile opposition as a result.

Sharp movements in the price of gold also have a direct impact on the international financial system. As we saw earlier, central banks have sought in recent years, through a more co-ordinated approach, to bring order to financial markets. This has involved them in sometimes agreeing to accept a certain amount of short-term instability in return for a new alignment that seems likely to provide some greater stability in the medium term. This was the thinking that lay behind the recent co-ordinated intervention to reduce the value of the American dollar.

Having said that, however, it must be emphasised that central banks interpret their main function as being to help to provide an environment of stability within which orderly international trade and capital flows can occur. Any proposal which invites them to play a role designed to have a de-stabilising effect (even if the objective of the destabilisation is an unpopular and repressive regime) is unlikely to meet with their favour.

The reasons for this can be emphasised by reflecting for a moment on the position in the world gold market of the Soviet Union. The USSR is the second-largest producer of gold. The amount of gold which it supplies to the world market fluctuates from year to year because it is such an important source of foreign revenue that the government seeks always to release it in a way that will maximise the return. It has never been in the West's interest for the gold price to so fluctuate that it either placed the Soviet Union under pressure for foreign exchange or allowed it to reap windfall profits. But if this was true in the past, how much more so is it now in the era of *glasnost*? Reports from recent summit meetings that President Gorbachev has held with various Western leaders indicate that the one element of assistance that the West can contribute to the delicate processes of institutional and eco-nomic reform in the Soviet Union have to do with the provision of a stable international environment. Gold is one critical element in that environment. Commercial bankers were almost unanimous in their view (where they held one on the subject) that the Soviet Union had been pursuing gold-market stability over the past few years, not seeking to force up the price, releasing gold onto the market in quantities and at times that contributed – if anything could – to relative stability. Crucial to the success of any such operation is its secrecy.

A proposal that Western governments and their central banks should embark on a public exercise of the same kind, with the strong probability that it would have an opposite effect to the one that was intended, would not make much of a contribution to the likely success of the reform movement in contemporary Russia.

And in any event, the proposal takes no account of what would happen if, in a situation in which a number of countries had imposed gold embargoes, and were selling from reserves to make up the shortfall, the South Africans did manage to put reasonably large quantities of gold into other parts of the market, say in the 'gold sponge' countries of Asia. Under these circumstances the extra volume of gold on the world market (or the mere rumour of it – the market price is deeply influenced by 'sentiment') would force down prices, once more diminishing the value of countries' reserves, undermining the profitability of other countries' gold production, and further disrupting the international financial system.

There are other difficulties with an embargo on South African gold. Those in favour of it point out that it would be necessary to distinguish between new South African gold (which would be embargoed) and old South African gold (which would not). But in practice there is no way of telling one from another.

Nor is it possible positively to identify the actual source of gold. It is true that all refined gold still contains traces of other elements, and that it is possible to identify the location of the origins of these elements by the process known as isotopic testing. But if gold from a reef in one part of the world is mixed in the process of refining with gold from two other reefs in two quite different parts of the world, then the origins of the bullion would have to remain forever obscure.

Nor in the current diverse state of international opinion about the importance of gold is it remotely likely that there could be the kind of international agreement on a gold sanction that would, ultimately, be essential to its success. No French politician, for instance, could possibly afford the public unpopularity that would be incurred in supporting a proposal for the French central bank to sell its gold reserves. As one French banker expressed it to us, 'We are rather fetishistic about gold'.

Whether the view is a fetish or not, some countries have

already expressed their opposition to sales of IMF gold in other contexts, and it cannot be too strongly emphasised that central banks are unlikely to put their gold stocks on the market in a public way and face the risk that the scheme would push prices down, reducing not only the proceeds from the sale but also the value of remaining stocks. And these stocks include not simply those of the country concerned, but of all other countries too, including the poor, less-developed countries that already have balance of payments difficulties and very thin reserves.

Seen in this light, the options available for reducing South Africa's earnings from gold do not look practical at this stage. We would question whether, in the light of the evidence produced in this chapter, they would be necessary even if they were practical. The fact is that through a combination of development, geology, domestic economic mismanagement in response to the ideology of apartheid, and the evolving international market, South African gold does not matter anything like as much as it used to, except for the white South African regime. In their current critical circumstances they need the contribution that gold used to make to their foreign currency reserves more badly than ever before. But the strong probability is that at long last the lode has run out. South African gold production is no longer sufficiently competitive for it to make the overwhelming contribution to the security of the apartheid regime that the regime had come to expect of it. Its leaders now seem reduced to simply praying that their troubles will be solved by an increase in the world price, but any reasonable assessment of the facts must conclude by judging that it is unlikely, in current circumstances, that the prayers will be answered.

As recently as 23 May 1989 the South African Minister of Finance, du Plessis, admitted to an audience composed of representatives of the South African Federation of Industry that South Africa had been operating abroad on a cash basis for sixteen consecutive quarters, and that he wondered whether any business enterprise could have existed in a similar way. He also revealed that South Africa had been close to closing its foreign exchanges in December 1988, and that it might have to take this course of action in June 1989. The only thing that could alleviate the situation, and help the country through the debt rescheduling problem of 1990, was a rapid rise in the price of gold. He concluded by appealing to business to hang on 'until we get our politics right'.

How international financial pressure can assist South Africans of all racial backgrounds to get their politics 'right', and what those politics might look like in the short term, are the difficult but absorbing topics of chapter eight.

Part III

International Financial Sanctions and the Eclipse of Apartheid

Of all the many measures that have been proposed, and in some cases implemented over the years to bring about the abolition of apartheid, the financial sanction that has been in place since August 1985 has undoubtedly placed more pressure on the regime than any other. In practical terms it has had the effect of restricting economic growth in South Africa by forcing a continuation of capital outflows, and compelling the regime to generate current account surpluses.

Low or negligible growth restricts the rate of job creation, which in turn means rapidly increasing rates of black unemployment. Recent fertility rates mean that the great bulk of this unemployment, progressively, is concentrated among young black people, many of whom, especially in the townships, already have good reason for being alienated from the regime. Collectively, these phenomena add up to a substantial portion of what white people in South Africa call 'the security problem'.

This problem feeds on itself through its effect on the economy, requiring ever higher levels of government expenditure for army and police, justice and prison institutions. The normal functioning of the domestic capital market has been inhibited by a complex system of official oversight and controls designed to prevent the flight of yet more domestic capital.

Higher public expenditure, however, means higher taxes

and/or more public borrowing. Whichever it is, it necessarily reduces the amount of savings available for domestic investment. This is a well-known problem in economic management: how much current consumption to forgo for investment in future production. The big problem for the regime in South Africa is that it considers it has no choice – a high level of government current spending is forced on it by security and other considerations that arise out of apartheid. As long as it clings to apartheid, and the financial sanction stays in place, its freedom of manoeuvre in this area will be steadily reduced. In our view the decision to seek a settlement in Namibia is one direct consequence of the regime's attempts to manage its way out of the dilemma. It is one of the ironies of the peace process in southern Africa that it owes its existence, at least in part, to the actions of Western bankers.

These things together have worked to undermine the confidence of many whites in South Africa, not least among the business and commercial communities, but also among the senior echelons of the public sector responsible for economic monitoring, reporting and management. Increasingly, through their public statements and actions, they have made it clear that they believe that the prospects for renewed growth and development in their country lie in political reform.

The decline in confidence imposes additional costs in political terms. Aware of the fragmentation of consensus about apartheid among its voters, the regime finds itself compelled to spend more to reassure and encourage support. This reaction adds to the burden of public expenditure and fuels inflation, making it self-defeating in even the short term, as these things further depress confidence.

The evidence is that the political and social imperatives of apartheid are a charge on the economy as a whole, inhibiting efficiency by misallocating resources, and introducing structural distortions. What has enabled apartheid to survive until now, despite rather than because of itself, has been its access to world stocks of capital, either through the sale of gold or through borrowing.

What the financial sanction has done is to reinforce tendencies that were already present in apartheid itself. Through this reinforcement their effects have been accelerated and multiplied. This is one ground for its very considerable success.

Another is the near-perfect unity with which it has been implemented. Again, this is because the financial sanction works with and not against tendencies inherent in the economy of international finance. South Africa is being excluded from the world stock of savings not because bankers and financiers are ideologically united in their detestation of apartheid – like the rest of the world, their views differ about its relative importance *vis-à-vis* other considerations (in their case such matters as shareholders' interests, or the legal requirements of banking procedure) – but because most of them now see South Africa as a bad risk. Its socio-economic circumstances do not make them confident that investments made there will be secure, so they are not able to recommend them to their shareholders.

As evidence of the accuracy of this judgement they point to the moratorium of 1985 which was imposed on them unilaterally by the South African authorities. The moratorium, and the two rescheduling agreements that have been reached since it was imposed, have had the effect of trapping commercial bank funds inside South Africa in direct opposition to the banks' wishes. Most of them had invested only in short-term securities precisely because they regarded longer terms as too risky. They are all still concerned to get their money out. Many have no inclination to lend again. Most are reinforced in this judgement by central banks, which have responsibility for the prudential management of the financial system in each domestic banking environment. The provisioning requirements for loans to South Africa that are being imposed by some central banks have raised the cost of lending to South African clients, and thus further deterred banks from making loans.

Many commercial banks in the Western world, with some notable exceptions in Europe, have also been profoundly influenced by public opinion. The pressures of local governments, university institutions, some commercial enterprises, churches, shareholders and clients, have all led banks to reassess the risks inherent in lending to South African entities. The threat of the loss of substantial domestic business as a consequence of engaging in South African lending has been an important deterrent.

So too, though more latterly, has been government intervention. In the United States, in the Nordic countries, in France and Italy, and in Japan, in some cases by legislation and in others by a combination of instruction and regulation, banks have been either prohibited or discouraged from lending to South Africa, either altogether, or at least in the medium to long term. In those countries where public opinion pressure is lower, where central bank provisioning requirements are less important, and where (unusually) a bank might take the view that investment in South Africa represented an acceptable risk – perhaps with a higher interest premium – government intervention has been playing an important role in restricting investment.

The effect of this combination of forces is to ensure that the financial sanction is almost ideal, because although in some cases backed up by governments, it is by and large a sanction that market forces work to encourage.

Two other features of the financial sanction that increase its impact relative to other sorts of measures are its ease of imposition and the consistent pressure it imposes on decision-makers and the political process. Both are worth considering in some detail.

The ease of imposition derives from the fact that financial sanctions are self-reinforcing. A decision by, say, a major car producer not to sell in South Africa improves the market share and profitability of other car producers, increasing their incentive to stay in that market. But a decision by a major bank, or group of banks, not to lend to South Africa is seen by other banks to make South Africa a poorer credit risk and a less attractive place in which to lend money.

Financial sanctions also impose enormous constraints on the

key decision-makers in South Africa. They limit the room for manoeuvre of the bureaucrats responsible for trying to ensure rational macro-economic management; the heads of state enterprises with investment and expansion plans, and the directors and managers of private sector firms that badly need capital for growth and development. These are precisely the people whose influential support is crucial for the government in the pursuit of its other policies.

We are convinced that the withdrawal of that support is in some measure occurring as a result of the financial sanction, and that it is contributing more than any other factor to the growth of demands for reform and the abolition of apartheid.

Financial sanctions are also important at the broader political level. Because the lack of foreign capital inflows compels the regime to seek to run a surplus on its balance of payments, economic policy has to be restrictive. Monetary policy has to be tight and interest rates have to be higher than they could otherwise be. Public expenditure and the budget deficit have to be better controlled. If applied consistently, however, this policy would hurt the white constituency, whose standards of living would necessarily fall, thereby also reducing their confidence in and support for the government. In practice the regime has not been able to follow restrictive policies consistently. As we have seen, when macro policy has been eased the current account surplus needed to repay debt has quickly contracted. This has demonstrated internationally the vulnerability of South Africa and further undermined the confidence of the elites whose interest lies in rational management of available resources.

Financial sanctions also put pressure on the black population. The scarcity of investment capital and slow economic growth result in slow job growth, which inevitably has its greatest impact on the black community where unemployment is already very great. One consequence of this, however, is the rapid growth of the informal sector, a subject in which South Africans of all racial communities are now taking some interest.

Growth in the informal sector is growth in economic opportunity for black people. It occurs more or less in isolation from the tradeable commodities sector of the international economy, so probably has little impact on the balance of payments. It provides employment and thus attracts more people towards it. As it grows, two consequences become apparent. First, various aspects of the repressive regulatory environment of apartheid are revealed to the people themselves as impediments to their present and future economic well-being. Secondly, these aspects of apartheid are also undermined, because they are not compatible with the development of a modern, industrial economy. People moved by want and ambition, encouraged by declining confidence among their historic oppressors and increasing direct assistance from people in the formal sector of the economy who believe that the 'internal development' of the informal sector offers hope of a way out of the impasse of apartheid, are less and less inclined to obey the laws which they have had no part in making, and which are against their economic interests. Financial sanctions are thus almost certainly, in a limited way, helping black people in South Africa to mount their own direct challenge to apartheid through the economy itself.

For these reasons we believe that the financial sanction should be maintained, and if possible tightened. We also believe that it must be done in a purposeful way to have as much direct impact on the South African balance of payments as possible. What might this mean in practice?

There are three ways in which the current embargo on international finance to South Africa might be strengthened: by tightening the conditions for debt repayment in the period after June 1990 when the present arrangements expire; by a consolidation of the embargo on medium- and long-term lending, and by an extension of the embargo to include short-term credits (mainly trade related). We examine each of these in turn.

Tightening the Conditions for Debt Repayment

The scope for achieving faster debt repayment is limited. As we saw earlier, the banks have very little freedom of manoeuvre in what they can demand and reasonably expect to get. By introducing the moratorium in the first place South Africa indicated its intention to behave unilaterally, and as far as the rescheduling discussions are concerned, this remains an option that is available to it. The money is in the 'net', and the pace at which it will be released is something that the South African authorities will decide. However, it remains in the regime's interest to try to come to an accommodation that is acceptable to the banks, since it hopes to be able to borrow again from world capital markets at the earliest possible time. We believe the banks should be encouraged (by their governments, shareholders, and public generally) to use what leverage they have to press for repayments at the highest rate.

In this regard we noted in chapter four that the second rescheduling, in 1987, involved a slowdown in capital repayments compared with the first rescheduling in 1986. This slowdown probably reflected a pessimistic view on the part of South African officials that the balance of payments was unlikely to improve sufficiently to make a greater commitment possible. The probability is that they will take the same pessimistic view in 1990, and that it will not take very long in negotiations to discover their bottom line.

Beyond that there is not a great deal to negotiate. There is no point in refusing to do a deal, because South Africa might then choose to default altogether. This would have the effect of liberating it from having to make any repayments at all, which would in turn alleviate the pressure on its balance of payments. Since this is precisely what we (and those seeking the end of apartheid inside South Africa) wish to avoid it would not make sense to encourage the banks to pursue such a strategy. A default would also have the effect of imposing costs on the banks (which would pass them on to their clients) because they would almost certainly be compelled to declare the loans non-performing and embark on the pursuit of expensive legal remedies in competition with each other.

Defaulting would not be entirely cost free for the South Africans either, a fact which they know, and which has encouraged them to embark on the series of rescheduling negotiations. For one thing it would seriously disrupt all of their credit transactions abroad. For a time at least South African traders would probably lose all access to trade finance and be forced to resort to cash or barter trading. It would also do further damage to their already poor long-term prospects of regaining access to international sources of credit.

A Consolidation of the Embargo on Medium- and Long-Term Lending

There is rather more scope in this proposal. The two key features of the financial isolation of South Africa are that it has been progressive and that it has been brought about largely as a result of market processes and grass-roots pressure activity, and not (until rather more recently) by the edicts of governments. One after another individual lenders have closed their doors to South Africa, and one by one major international corporations have disinvested, or ceased looking to South Africa for business.

While profitability in South Africa has played some part in this, so too have questions of worldwide profitability, as markets elsewhere are lost as a result of being involved in South Africa in the first place. There are no examples of banks or international enterprises which have decided to pull out of South Africa reversing that decision, and there seems little reason to expect that any will do so. The medium-term economic outlook is far from attractive. The state of unrest and political conflict is a clear disincentive. Those businesses that have withdrawn in response to customer and shareholder pressures are hardly likely to go back until a change in local conditions in South Africa persuades those doing the pressurising to desist.

None the less, the South African authorities and financial

community are still investing considerable resources in trying to maintain friendly relations with international sources of finance. Major banks in Western Europe, the United Kingdom, Japan and even the United States (where the law prohibits most lending to South African residents) still receive high-level delegations from South African financial institutions, and Western bankers continue to visit South Africa.

At the moment countries with banks which might do new business with South African entities differ in their approach both to how much may be lent and for how long. Some have legislation (the United States, the Nordic countries, Malaysia), some have government regulation (France, Italy, Switzerland), some enforce provisioning through their financial authorities (Federal Republic of Germany, Canada, the United Kingdom) and some successfully employ persuasion (Japan, Australia).

We do not believe that all countries should have and enforce exactly the same embargo provisions. We accept that banking systems, and the levels of government intervention in them, differ from country to country.

Without interfering in these areas it would in our view be of help if there were rather more transparency in the arrangements, so that the public could know more precisely what the local policies regarding South Africa were, and the extent to which they were being implemented. To achieve this, constant monitoring of the situation in each country, with regular publication, would be an advantage. We were impressed with the extent to which banks were acutely conscious of the importance of public opinion in shaping their attitudes towards South African business. In permitting public opinion to be better informed, and more able to apply intelligent pressure, a transparency agency would be a welcome addition to the machinery of anti-apartheid politics.

In our view this would also be helpful to individual banks and countries who currently find themselves, unfairly, under suspicion of providing medium- and long-term loan finance to South African entities. Switzerland, Taiwan, the Republic of Korea and Japan could all benefit in this way.

Monitoring may not be easy. An attempt by the IRRC (Cooper 1988b) to survey the top 100 non-US banks about their lending policy towards South Africa, had only a poor response rate, which suggested that banks were unwilling to impart this sort of information. We believe that monitoring can be effective if: it is carried out by a body that clearly understands international banking and is sympathetic to its objectives; it occurs regularly, so that institutions that refuse to co-operate become known to the public; it is conducted in a clearly impartial manner. Under these conditions we would expect that most banks would come to see what many already believe, that it is in their interests that there should be clear public understanding of their policy position on South African lending.

Increased public information and awareness would also provide opportunities for the public endorsement of what in the nature of things must remain private diplomatic pressure. We are aware that the United States has brought pressure to bear on Japan to encourage it not to provide finance for apartheid, and that it has also influenced Taiwan (though not necessarily for the same reason) to get its central bank to moderate its gold acquisition program. We think that there should be a rather greater diplomatic effort to draw the rapidly growing economies of the Far East into the shared Western active disapproval of apartheid. This is particularly the case with regard to Taiwan and the Republic of Korea. In addition, the United Kingdom could make more of a diplomatic effort in this regard in Hong Kong. These efforts might help to ensure that the rapidly expanding capital markets of the Far East were closed to South African borrowers, just as are the established markets of Western Europe and North America.

A transparency agency, bringing information to the attention of a wide international audience of concerned citizens, would make a practical contribution to creating the conditions in which this diplomacy might be brought to bear.

The Extension of the Sanction to Include Trade Finance

South African access to medium- and long-term trade credits (in excess of two years) is already very heavily constrained. Should short-term trade credits be included in the sanction?

While trade credits cannot provide a permanent solution to South Africa's foreign capital requirements they can provide (and have done so) a safety net to cover short-term balance of payments difficulties. Additional resort to trade credits can provide foreign funds to help meet debt repayments abroad in the event that the current account surplus and South Africa's small reserves of foreign exchange and gold are insufficient. This enables the authorities to pursue higher growth policies, taking more risks of periodic external account difficulties. In the event of payments problems arising, the authorities would simply need to advise importers that goods would not be cleared unless payment was covered by a credit of say one year or more, rather than the normal ninety days.

It must be stressed, however, that trade credits are not a viable instrument for South Africa to obtain the sustained access to capital resources which it must have in order to restrict further growth in unemployment. Special efforts to lift the flow or maturity of short-term trade credits might produce an inflow of funds in a particular period. However this would be followed by an outflow as the credits were repaid, unless the special efforts were sustained indefinitely.

Furthermore, South Africa's current access to short-term trade credits is limited. Many banks will not do even this type of business with South African residents, and because the 1985 moratorium demonstrated that even short-term loans were vulnerable to unilateral rescheduling, limits on how much trade-credit business may be conducted have been reduced in most countries, and are fully enforced.

None the less, it seems to us that rather more could be done in this field.

In our view it would make sense to allow the market to accept rather more of the risk. There seems no good reason why, in the current state of its internal socio-political relations, South Africa should be 'on cover' for short-term trade credits in official export-credit agencies. All that this does, in the case of loss, is to transfer the restitution costs, indirectly, to the taxpaying public of the country concerned. If banks and other credit agencies had to accept the full risk involved in advancing trade credits for South African business, and thus had to pay the higher insurance premiums in the private market, the cost of trade-credit finance would be higher, and its pattern would probably be rather different.

For a start not all trade-credit business involving trade to and from South Africa would come to an end. Banks would continue to be able to service their own clients' trade with South Africa if they chose to do so (mainly supplier credits but some buyer credits too), while it would become somewhat harder for South African exporters to gain access to international trade finance. Such a change should have less impact on the flow of imports into South Africa than on the flow of exports from the Republic, thus contributing to a deterioration in South Africa's visible trade balance.

For these reasons, and as a next step, we would recommend that all official export credit agencies take South Africa 'off cover' for all trade credits.

Apart from loan finance and trade credits, the other ways in which capital flows into South Africa are through gold purchases and swaps, and via the market for equity investments and bonds.

The equity market, and how it is serviced by international banks, particularly in New York, is a lively and intricate subject, worthy of a monograph of its own. In terms of South Africa's capital requirements, however, it is of negligible importance, and is certainly not of sufficient size to make any real contribution to the solution of South Africa's underlying problem: a balance of payments constraint on its capacity for growth. Occasional statistical evidence of the movement of R73 or 75 million onto the Johannesburg stock exchange from

international sources may indicate that small investors see
opportunities for profit from movements in the financial Rand
exchange rate, but they do nothing to shore up the sagging
base of the economy as a whole. We think they are irrelevant
in practical economic terms, and should be ignored. Morality
is another matter, which each investor must decide for itself.
However, so long as it remains the policy of Western democracies to permit investment in South African securities by their
nationals, it follows that correspondent banking facilities
should be available. We have not collected evidence for this
study on either the volume or importance of correspondent
banking business to and from South Africa, though we are
conscious that it is an area of some concern to thoughtful
elements in the anti-apartheid movement inside South Africa
itself. In our view, correspondent banking activity, which
includes business arising from movements of capital out of
South Africa, as well as emigration by South African residents,
would be a worthwhile area for further research.

Gold is a far more important subject. We have already
devoted considerable space to explaining why we believe that
a sanction on South African gold is impractical. Here we should
add that in our view any attempt to impose an international
embargo on South African gold would simply shift the trade
into the world of organised crime. This would not be in the
interests of anyone.

All of this has concentrated on capital flows into South
Africa. Part of the regime's difficulty with capital flows also
relates to the fact that there is capital flight from South Africa
that is in addition to the money being transferred for the
repayment of debt.

Some of this capital flight is from the process of disinvestment by international companies, and we have explained in
chapter six how this works and what it involves. The debate
about licensing and royalty payments is growing audibly,
particularly in the United States. Should disinvesting companies make such agreements? Our general impression is that their
effect in economic terms is neutral in the short to medium term.

That is that the benefits to the regime of preserving the contacts which licensing deals involve, are fairly evenly balanced by the drain on the balance of payments which they also entail. Over the medium to long term, however, we would expect this neutral effect to become a small advantage to the regime. This is because of the potential for future technology and management skill transfers which licensing arrangements entail. Thus, where you stand on this issue might depend on your evaluation of how much longer apartheid is likely to last.

As far as disinvestment *per se* is concerned, we are confident that the pressure of public opinion in the home countries of the corporations concerned is a major determinant of the decision to disinvest, and that as long as this pressure continues to be exerted further disinvestment will occur.

The major part of the departing capital, however, does not come from foreign companies disinvesting. It is indigenous South African money fleeing the country. This includes personal savings invested abroad by individuals who have lost confidence in the domestic economy.

Rather more important is capital exported to enable smaller businesses to hedge their positions more effectively. Typically it goes into the purchase or creation of small overseas subsidiaries. We have explained earlier how this can facilitate the systematic export of capital at the commercial Rand exchange rate. Of even greater significance are the large sums being exported by big South African corporations to purchase foreign assets, and so diversify their activities and reduce their dependence on South African business.

The growing involvement of large South African corporations outside the Republic has prompted the question of whether it is appropriate for banks to lend to these offshoots of South African business. The question has arisen in a controversial way recently in connection with the unsuccessful bid by Minorco – an international company controlled by the South African Anglo-American Corporation – to take over Consolidated Gold Fields Plc, a London-based company with extensive holdings in various mineral extracting industries.

There was some criticism of the Canadian Bank of Nova Scotia for having made extensive credit available to Minorco to enable it to bid for Consgold.

The Minorco takeover proposal has run into a number of difficulties around the world. There have been strategic and anti-monopoly concerns arising from the prospect that a very large part of Western production of certain minerals could come under the control of one entity and that the entity concerned was South African controlled. There has also been concern at the impact of the proposed takeover on minority shareholders and on proposed ventures in countries which prohibit commercial contact with South Africa.

These are all legitimate concerns to which governments need have regard in determining their reactions to the proposed takeover.

We have put all those issues specific to the Minorco bid to one side and examined the general issue of lending to South African Corporations operating outside the Republic.

The issue is a complex one and demands careful thought. For a start, under the rules of the OECD it is not possible for any member country to deny to a foreign-owned company incorporated within its territory the same trading opportunities as are available to local companies (the non-discrimination principle). This effectively means that a bank loan to a South African entity established in any one of the twenty-four member countries of the OECD cannot be prevented by government intervention in that country.

This does not mean, however, that South African companies that have started businesses in foreign countries, and taken out loans, are free to transfer the capital thus acquired back to South Africa. As far as the great majority of big loans are concerned, banks lend the money, under contract, for specific purposes. Where the banks or the relevant monetary authorities have placed an embargo on lending to South Africa, those purposes could not include the application of the finance thus acquired to projects inside South Africa. Of course there are ways in a which a corporation can surreptitiously transfer funds from one country to another. While such transfers can be difficult for government authorities to detect, quantify and prove, there would be a considerable risk that the financial community would become aware of them. Accordingly, we would not expect large enterprises seeking to establish their credentials in a by-and-large suspicious outside world to risk major capital transfers of this kind.

What is more interesting is the question of whether South African companies outside South Africa should be eligible for loans for the purchase and development of other companies. Normally such loans would only be advanced to companies which were putting up some of their own funds for the purchase. These would be either funds being exported from South Africa or funds otherwise available for repatriation to South Africa. Thus the takeover would involve a drain on South African capital, and with it might well go entrepreneurial skills and commitment. These developments will have the effect of further weakening South Africa's balance of payments and its longer-term prospects for growth and employment.

For the moment, we believe the main motivation of South African companies looking for overseas investment opportunities is as a means of escaping from the threatening socio-political climate at home. Far from easing South Africa's domestic economic problems, they are making them worse. Each decision to invest outside the country is an investment forgone inside it. Companies that make profits from foreign operations do not seem inclined to repatriate them, preferring to retain the earnings outside South Africa as a hedge against further economic deterioration and political turbulence. For those who wish to see apartheid overthrown, these are matters to be encouraged.

As we noted in chapter five, the South African authorities assess proposed investments abroad on a case-by-case basis. Investments seen as important to the development or protection of strategic trade links are actively encouraged. It is appropriate for opponents of apartheid to take these factors into account in assessing particular proposals.

The Eclipse of Apartheid

We saw earlier that the United States Congress enacted legislation in 1983 that effectively prevents the US director of the IMF from supporting any proposal to lend money to South Africa. The United States has similar legislation aimed at communist regimes. We should not be too surprised. The apartheid of South Africa and the communism of the Soviet Union have a number of things in common. Both have, for ideological reasons, created highly regulated economies, with directed labour and capital markets. Both have, out of fear of the outside world, sought to protect themselves from external threat with a buffer of client states, whose economies are tied into the same infrastructure. Both have, historically, displayed a sort of paranoia about the evil intentions of outside interferers that would be comic but for the threat it has posed to international security. Both have contrived to create nightmare economies in which waste has become a prominent feature.

Recovery from the disadvantages imposed by these mistaken policy orientations depends heavily on being able to generate sufficient internal political dynamism to ensure that meaningful reform can occur without crippling social turbulence. Both the Soviet Union and South Africa seem now to have entered a phase of their history in which their different capacities for this difficult task are being tested.

South Africa's problems are terrible, and it is as well to remind ourselves of this fact. There has been a tendency among those of us who detest apartheid to speak as if its destruction will automatically solve South Africa's problems. The truth is, rather, that even if South Africa had been practising the democratic method for the past sixty years, it would still have enormous social problems. The transition from apartheid to democracy, important as it unquestionably is, will mark only the beginning of a new phase in which large and difficult issues will need to be addressed.

We mention this because the embargo on finance to South Africa exists for a purpose; it is not an end in itself. Once the institutions of apartheid have been abolished we would expect to see financial sanctions lifted. This will not be uniformly easy to achieve. Sanctions of the sort imposed by the United States Congress in its Comprehensive Anti-Apartheid Act, though it may not always seem so, are relatively easy to impose and to enforce, and relatively difficult to lift once their usefulness has expired.

That the usefulness of financial sanctions will expire should not be doubted. We mention this because there has been considerable discussion among bankers over what reforms South Africa would have to introduce in order to requalify for access to world financial markets. We questioned bankers on this issue and discovered a low but it seemed to us real level of consensus. Many of them mentioned a particular sequence of actions that constituted a minimum agenda for reasonably rapid transformation. These were:

• the release of political prisoners, and in particular the leadership cadres of the main black political organisations;
• the unbanning of those organisations so that they could resume their work as articulators and representatives of black political interests;
• the lifting of the state of emergency so that that work could begin to take practical expression in meetings and discussions;
• the beginning of meaningful negotiations over a new constitution.

What these negotiations would involve is a matter for the South African people themselves, but at a minimum it is hard to imagine them beginning without:

(a) a clear commitment to an end to all violence, including white coercive repression in excess of normal policing;

(b) an agenda, however loosely phrased; and

(c) a time-frame within which all the parties to the negotiations agree that they should be largely complete.

Our view is that international bankers would accept a package of this kind, and we think that their acceptance ought to constitute sufficient grounds for readmitting South Africa to the international stock of savings which are of such importance to its future development. Those who are anxious to see the destruction of apartheid would also, we expect, wish to ensure that economic growth rates closer to those that were being achieved in South Africa in the 1960s should begin again as soon as possible, since their benefits will flow more rapidly to the black population in a post-apartheid economy.

It is also our firm impression that a basis already exists for the actual form that the difficult negotiations might take. The South African Law Commission's working paper on 'Group and Human Rights', prepared under the direction of Mr Justice Oliver, sets out both a scrupulous recognition of the importance of individual rights in the framework of any democratic constitution and also proposes a negotiating method for arriving at a constitutional settlement in which individual human rights would occupy a central place. Without endorsing these specific proposals as necessarily the ones to be adopted, we are encouraged by their existence to believe that the apparent development of a serious mood for far-reaching reform is increasingly matched in the reality of South African political life.

For the sake of all South Africans, let us hope so.

References

Anti-Apartheid Movement (1988). *The South African Disconnection.* London, April.

Apter, David (1971). *Choice and the Politics of Allocation.* New Haven: Yale University Press.

Barry, Brian (1965). *Political Argument.* London: Routledge & Kegan Paul.

Baynham, Simon (1987). 'Political Violence and the Security Response'. In Jesmond Blumenfeld (ed.), *South Africa in Crisis,* London: Croom Helm for the Royal Institute of International Affairs, 1987, pp. 107–25.

Bell, Daniel (1973). *The Coming of Post-Industrial Society.* New York: Basic Books.

Blumenfeld, Jesmond (1987a). 'Economy Under Siege'. In Jesmond Blumenfeld (ed.), *South Africa in Crisis,* London: Croom Helm for the Royal Institute of International Affairs, 1987, pp. 17–33.

Blumenfeld, Jesmond (ed.) (1987b). *South Africa in Crisis.* London: Croom Helm for the Royal Institute of International Affairs.

Boulding, Kenneth E. (1978). *Ecodynamics: A New Theory of Societal Evolution.* London: Sage.

Brown, Mike (1988). *The Gold Market 'Far Eastern Sponge'.* Johannesburg: Davis Borkum Hare Economic Research, October.

Brown, Mike (1989a). *World Gold Market: Supply and Demand Trends 1988 and 1989*. Johannesburg: Davis Borkum Hare Economic Research, January.

Brown, Mike (1989b). *The Outlook for the South African Gold Mining Industry*. Johannesburg: Davis Borkum Hare Economic Research, March.

Commonwealth Group of Eminent Persons (1986). *Mission to South Africa: The Commonwealth Report*. Harmondsworth: Penguin.

Cooper, Alison (1988a). *International Business in South Africa 1988*. Washington, DC: Investor Responsibility Research Centre, June.

Cooper, Alison (1988b). *International Bank Lending to South Africa: A Survey of the Top 100 Non-U.S. Banks*, Washington, DC: Investor Responsibility Research Centre, September.

Cooper, Alison (1989). *U.S. and Canadian Business in South Africa 1989*. Washington, DC: Investor Responsibility Research Centre, January.

Dahrendorf, Ralf (1968). *Society and Democracy in Germany*. London: Weidenfeld & Nicolson.

George, Abraham M. and Giddy, Ian H. (1983). *International Finance Handbook*, New York: Wiley.

Giddens, Anthony (1973). *The Class Structure of Advanced Societies*. London: Hutchinson.

Gould, Stephen J. (1981). *The Mismeasure of Man*. Harmondsworth: Penguin.

Harris, Laurence (1986). 'South Africa's External Debt Crisis', *Third World Quarterly*, July.

Hauck, David (1986). *U.S. Corporate Withdrawal from South Africa: The Likely Impact on Political Change*. Washington, DC: Investor Responsibility Research Centre, August.

Hirsch, Alan (1989). Sanctions and the South African Economy. Mimeo.

Inter-governmental Group of Officials (1988). South Africa's Relationship with the International Financial System. Statement by the Commonwealth Committee of Foreign Ministers on Southern Africa, Toronto: Commonwealth Secretariat, mimeo. (The Financial Links Study)

Johnson, R. W. (1977). *How Long Will South Africa Survive?* London: Macmillan.

Keppel-Jones, Arthur (1968). *South Africa: A Short History*. London: Hutchinson, 4th edn.

Kibbe, Jennifer and Hauch, David (1988). *Leaving South Africa: the Impact of U.S. Corporate Disinvestment*. Washington, DC: Investor Responsibility Research Centre, July.

Koistinen, David J. and Lind, John E. (1988). *South Africa's Gold and Diamond Trade*. San Francisco: Cannicor Research, January.

Lanning, Greg, with Mueller, Marti (1979). *Africa Undermined: Mining Companies and the Underdevelopment of Africa*. Harmondsworth: Penguin.

La Porte, Todd (ed.) (1975). *Organised Social Complexity: Challenge to Politics and Policy*. Princeton: Princeton University Press.

Leach, Graham (1986). *South Africa: No Easy Path to Peace*. London: Routledge & Kegan Paul.

Lewis, S. R. (1987). *Economic Realities in Southern Africa (or, One Hundred Million Futures)*. Institute of Development Studies, discussion paper no. 232.

Lind, John E. and Koistinen, David J. (1988). *Financing South Africa's Foreign Trade*. San Francisco: Cannicor Research, March.

Lipset, Seymour Martin (1981). *Political Man: The Social Bases of Politics*. Baltimore: John Hopkins University Press, revised and expanded edn.

Lipton, Merle (1985). *Capitalism and Apartheid: South Africa, 1910-1986*. Aldershot: Wildwood House.

Lipton, Merle (1987). 'Reform: Destruction or Modernization of Apartheid?' In Jesmond Blumenfeld (ed.), *South Africa in Crisis*, London: Croom Helm for the Royal Institute of International Affairs, 1987, pp. 34-55.

Lipton, Merle (1988). *Sanctions and South Africa: The Dynamics of Economic Isolation*. London: Economist Intelligence Unit, special report no. 1119.

Lucas, J. L. (1976). *Democracy and Participation*. Harmondsworth: Penguin.

Pallister, David, Stewart, Sarah and Lepper, Ian (1988). *South Africa Inc.: The Oppenheimer Empire.*, New Haven: Yale University Press, revised edn.

Pringle, Robert (1982). *How Central Banks Manage Their Reserves.* New York: Group of Thirty, April.

Salant, Stephen W. (1988). Prepared Statement before the U.S. Congress House of Representatives sub-committee on Africa, Committee on Foreign Affairs. Washington, DC: 23 March.

Savage, Michael (1986). *The Cost of Apartheid.* Cape Town: University of Cape Town, new series pamphlet no. 121.

Steiner, George (1971). *In Bluebeard's Castle: Some Notes Towards the Redefinition of Culture.* London: Faber.

Thompson, Leonard (1985). *The Political Mythology of Apartheid.* New Haven: Yale University Press.

Touraine, Alain (1971). *The Post Industrial Society.* New York: Random House.

United Nations, Economic and Social Council (1989a). *Transnational Corporations in South Africa and Namibia.* New York: E/C.10/1989/8, 14 February.

United Nations, Economic and Social Council (1989b). *Transnational Corporations in South Africa and Namibia.* New York: E/C.10/1989/9, 22 February.

United Nations, Economic and Social Council (1989c). *Transnational Corporations.* New York: E/1989/17, 3 March.

United States General Accounting Office (1988). *South Africa: Trends in Trade, Lending and Investment.* Report to Congressional Requesters. Washington, DC: GAO/NSIAD-88-165, April.

Uys, Stanley (1987). 'Whither the White Oligarchy?' In Jesmond Blumenfeld (ed.), *South Africa in Crisis*, London: Croom Helm for the Royal Institute of International Affairs, 1987, pp. 56-76.

Wilson, Christopher (1987). 'South Africa's Debt Overhang'. *Optima* 35 (2), June.

Wilson, Francis and Ramphele, Mamphela (1989). *Uprooting Poverty: The South African Challenge.* Report for the Second

Carnegie Inquiry into Poverty and Development in Southern Africa. New York: W. W. Norton & Co.

World Gold Commission (1988). *The Italian Jewellery Industry
Apartheid's Biggest Customer*. London. Mimeo, November.

World Gold Commission (1989?). *The Case for a Gold Sanction in
the Fight Against Apartheid*. London.

Index

FOR THE BEST IN PAPERBACKS, LOOK FOR THE 🐧

PENGUIN

Shouting from China Helene Chung

Helene Chung, Australian journalist born of ethnic Chinese parents, describes her term as the Australian Broadcasting Corporation's Beijing correspondent.

Based on the daily life of a foreign correspondent in Beijing, it gives a vivid portrait of China today – China's attitude to overseas Chinese, its dilemma in wanting to modernise through the importation of western technology without the importation of western ideas, and the problems of adequately reporting to the world on a vast country which is still such an enigma.

Katherine Mansfield Gillian Boddy

Katherine Mansfield was not only an extraordinary writer, devoted to her work, she was also a woman of great vivacity and strength, who led a brief but fascinating life from her birth in New Zealand to the literary circles of England and Europe. The leading writers of her age, people like Virginia Woolf and D. H. Lawrence, were a constant part of her life.

Gillian Boddy has drawn on her years of research to introduce to us a new Katherine Mansfield, not ethereal as has been the myth, but substantial, alive.

Shalom Compiled by Nancy Keesing

Some of the fourteen prominent contributors to this unique collection of stories – John George Lang, Harry Marks and Nancy Keesing herself – come from long-established Australian Jewish families. Others like Judah Waten, David Martin, Morris Lurie and Lilian Barnea are refugees of pogroms, revolutions and wars.

By drawing upon the diversity of their backgrounds and inspirations, well-known author and critic Nancy Keesing gives us an invaluable insight into Jewish life and thought in contemporary Australia.

Old Worlds and New Australia Janis Wilton and Richard Bosworth

This topical book provides an overview of Australia's immigration policy since World War II: its impact on attitudes and lifestyles in Australia, as well as upon those who have brought to the new world their memories, dreams and conflicts.

A Foreign Wife Gillian Bouras

In 1980 Australian-born Gillian Bouras set off with her Greek husband to live in Greece. Her fellow villagers fondly regarded her, a migrant in their midst, as something of a curiosity. They in turn were the source of admiration and curiosity to her. This is her account of her experience in a 'small quiet world' which caused her so much perplexity and pleasure.

Don't Take Your Love to Town Ruby Langford

Ruby Langford was born on Bos Ridge mission, Coraki, on the north coast of NSW in 1934. She was raised in Bonalbo, and went to high school in Casino where she finished second form. At age 15 she moved to Sydney and became a qualified clothing machinist. Her first child was born when she was 17. She has a family of nine children and raised them mostly by herself. For many years she lived in tin huts and camped in the bush around Coonabarrabran, working at fencing, burning off, ringbarking and lopping, and pegging kangaroo skins. At other times she lived in the black areas of Sydney and worked in clothing factories. Now 53, she is the grandmother of eighteen children, and works part-time at the Aboriginal Medical Service in Redfern.

The Penguin History of Australia   John Molony

A history for the people which is an enticing and comprehensive blend of social, political, cultural, economic and environmental history. Included are those so often neglected by historians, the 'ordinary' Australians whose class, race, age or gender rendered them 'unimportant'.

Here is the story of the making of a nation, the slow and painful process by which a people have come to identify with each other and with the land they inhabit. It tells of strangers and of the strange land which they encountered, confronted and, ultimately, came to understand and respect.

While John Molony deals with the strength of the British heritage, he is keenly aware of the richness resulting from its blending with other cultures. Although Molony is not blind to the failures and follies which followed the white peopling of Australia, his thoughtful and timely history is an acknowledgement of the considerable achievements of 200 years.

The Penguin Book of Australian Autobiography   John and Dorothy Colmer

A lively and stimulating introduction to more than forty Australians who write of their own lives. They include Kylie Tennant, Patrick White, Joan Lindsay, David Malouf, Henry Lawson, Judah Waten, Charles Perkins, Donald Horne, Albert Facey, Clive James, George Johnston and Mary Gilmore.